A Study of the Supply Chain and Financial Parameters of a Small Business

----A Case Study of a Factory in Karnataka, India

by

Rahul Basu

IV Semester MBA

Reg. No. MBA15183

Project Report submitted to the University of Mysore in partial fulfillment of the Requirements of IV Semester MBA degree examinations   June 2017

University of Mysore, Manasagangothri,
Mysore -570006

ACKNOWLEDGEMENT

A word of thanks to all those people who helped me to bring out this internship project report.

My thanks to Mr. Kulkarni DGM head of the production maintenance Department in SSS Pvt ltd for offering me this specialized opportunity to do this internship training. My heartfelt thanks to Mr Jawad Basith and Omer Basith Director and CEO of Solid State Systems for allowing me to pursue the study.

I extend my regards to all the employees and workers who gave me great support to carry out this report

Rahul Basu

Solid State Systems Private Limited

No. 38A-1, KIADB Industrial Area, Hoskote, Bangalore - 562 114, India
Phone : +91-80-27971145 / 1148 / 1149   Fax : +91-80-27971146
E-mail : ssspl@vsnl.com   Internet : http://www.syscapindia.com.
CIN : U51909KA1972PTC002179.

Dt. 04.09.2017

CERTIFICATE

This is to certify that Dr. RAHUL BASU has conducted a study of our systems and the working of our factory during the period July – August 2017.

For SOLID STATE SYSTEMS PVT LTD.

Director.

Dedicated to

My beloved parents.

CONTENTS

CHAPTER	TITLE	PAGE
	Certificate	(i)
	Company Certificate	(ii)
	Declaration	(iii)
	Acknowledgement	(iv)
	Contents	(v)
	List of Tables	(vi)
	List of Figures/Charts	(vii)
	List of Abbreviations	(viii)
I	Introduction	10
II	Findings	28
III	Functioning of various Departments	31
	• Finance	
	• Production	
	• Marketing	
	• HR	
	• Production	
	Product Profile	
IV	SWOT Analysis Conclusion Appendices	75

LIST OF TABLES

3.1   Span of Control

Ratio analysis

Salary scales

Incentives and bonus

Balance sheet 2015

Loans

Profit and Loss

LIST OF FIGURES/CHARTS

Fig 1. Factory entrance Salary scales PRODUCTION DEPARTMENT SALARIES

Fig 2.1. Organization chart Salary scales HEADS OF VARIOUS DEPARTMENTS

Fig 3.2.1 Structure of Finance function

Fig 3.3.1 Structure of Production

Fig 3.3.2 Structure under Head of Production

Fig 3.5.1 PPC system

Fig 3.5.2 Typical job card

Fig 3.5.3 Job order card

Fig 3.5.4 Sample job card

Fig 3.5.5 Route card

Fig 3.7.1 Marketing structure

Fig 4.1.1 Flow Chart

Fig 4.1.2 Built-in Quality checks

Fig 4.1.3 Quality Assurance Process

Fig 4.1.4 Metallization unit

Fig 4.1.5 Winding unit

Fig 4.4.1 Activity dimensions for Supply Chain

Fig 4.4.2 Supply chain Components

Fig 4.6.1 Representative products

Fig 4.6.2 General Technical Specifications

Fig 4.6.3 typical specifications for P 100 series

Figs 5.1,5.2,5.3 salary vs. level for various departments

LIST OF ABBREVIATIONS

Takt : a time standard in production

SSPL Solid State Systems Pvt Ltd

SWOT : strengths weaknesses, opportunities, threats

MTBF: Mean time between failures

GST: goods and services tax

CEO chief executive Officer

CPA   Chartered Public Accountant

VAT   Value added tax

SAP   software manufacturer

ERP Enterprise Resource Planning

JIT Just in Time

MTBF Mean Time between Failures

PERT Project evaluation reporting Technique

PP&C Production Planning and Control

GM General Manager

QC Quality Control

a cost of ordering per order

B batch size

I inventory carry cost per unit per unit time

p non dim ratio

q Q/Q_m

Q Quantity

S Demand

Z normalized score

ATA average total assets

CCD cash to cycle time

DPO days of payment outstanding

DSO days of sales outstanding

TID total inventory days

TO Turnover percentage

ROE return on equity

ROI return on investment

SHE share holder equity

NS net sales

NP Net Profit

INTRODUCTION

I PROBLEM DEFINITION

The country's emphasis on self-reliance and entry into the global market has made it imperative to adopt and follow lean and ethical management practices. In order to maintain viability and profitability in view of various global players and competition from the tigers of S.E Asia, the industry has to incorporate the tools and practices followed internationally. Local companies have been encouraged to enter the field with the indigenization "Make in India" policies of the Government. However, their competitiveness and survival in the market depend on various factors involving Productivity, Management, Lean Manufacturing, and Finance. The know-how gained in this MBA course gave tools whereby the parameters obtained in the study could be analyzed. A local company was chosen for testing some of these concepts.

COMPANY PROFILE

SOLID STATE SYSTEMS (P) LTD was incorporated in 1972 with the objective of manufacturing capacitors. It manufactures Metallized Polypropylene Film Capacitors used in domestic appliances, as well as metallized Polypropylene film, Polyurethane resin and Aluminum Cans.

The unit, located at Plot No.38 A-1, KIADB Industrial Area, Hoskote, Bangalore- 562 114 has all the necessary plant, machinery and test equipment to manufacture high-quality Metallized Film Capacitors (present capacity 12..0 mn. Pcs/ year), Metallized Polypropylene film (500 M.T. per year), P.U.Resin (1000 MT per year).

Solid State Systems has had its Quality Systems has been certified for ISO 9001-2000.and is certified under OSHAS. Solid State Systems has got UL Safety Certification for its Product as well as TUV Certification.

MANAGEMENT:

The company is managed by its Managing Director under the supervision of its Board of Directors supported by a qualified and experienced team of professionals looking after the day-to-day operations of the company.

Managing Director of the Company is an Engineer (Manchester University), with 12 years experience. He has overseen the Technical aspects of the Company (Production, Quality Assurance) as well as Commercial functions (Marketing and Purchase) before assuming the post of Managing Director.

COMPANY OWNERSHIP STRUCTURE :

The shareholding of the company is closely held by the Directors and their families.

4. PRODUCTS & APPLICATION

Solid State Systems manufactures capacitors used in the following applications:

Single phase motors, single phase pumps, air conditioners, washing machines, lighting appliances and in power electronic application

Metalized Polypropylene Film, Aluminum cans and P U Resin manufactured are used in capacitor manufacture.

5. MARKET

DOMESTIC

The Company is primarily an OEM supplier and among the major customers are CRI, Chola Pumps, Best Engineers, Sharp Industries, Carrier Aircon, Voltas, Kirloskar Brothers, GE Motors, Lubi Pumps, Godrej Washing Machines, Emerson etc. The company has long-standing relations with most of its customer base and enjoys strong customer loyalty as it has grown with its customers and has supported them with competitive pricing, timely delivery, and reliable quality.

The company markets its capacitors directly and also through the sales depots in Coimbatore, Faridabad & Selling Agents in Mumbai & Dewas. Regular trips to stay in touch with customers and the market are made by the Directors and Sales personnel.

OVERSEAS:

The company exports to Sri Lanka, Singapore, Thailand, Malaysia, Philippines, Saudi Arabia, UAE, South Africa, Spain, Czech Republic and Slovakia. Exports constitute about 30% of the company's turnover.

Figure 1: Factory Entrance

II Research Objectives

The objectives of this study were to review the operations of a local company engaged in export-oriented activities and illustrate adherence to and deficiencies of typical management principles applicable to such activities. In particular, it was attempted to show whether such principles were followed in letter as well as practice.

Objective 1: Evaluate the structure of the company

This objective is addressed by studying the organization chart and connectivity within the company, with the span of control and vertical chain of command.

Objective 2: Evaluate the salary structure and HR practices of the company

Data for salaries is examined using various analytical tools.

Objective 3: Evaluate the profitability and financial status of the company

This is accomplished by studying various parameters and ratios derived from the balance sheets.

Objective 4: Evaluate the Productivity of the company

Using the results of the ratios, tools from SCM are applied to derive the cash and turnover ratios.

III Research Methodology

The study does not purport to be an in-depth study of the organization, as this would have taken much more time than the brief duration allotted as well as the reluctance of the management to disclose particulars of financial and operational dealings for various reasons, implied or unknown. However, on face value, the study showed adherence to as well as defects of various management and operational norms.

Since most of the processes are automated, the methodology used is to work on established data and benchmarks relevant to the industry. These are averages over large numbers of items produced over different time spans.

Financial ratios and outlays for various expenditures are extracted from the financial reports of the company.

Next, the Supply Chain Performance is evaluated by various methods from these figures. The results can then be compared with industry benchmarks.

Chapterisation: The report has various chapters covering the company profile (II), functioning of various departments (III) and conclusion (IV) along with tables and charts.

IV Limitations of the Project Study.

Since this is a study comprising the main functions and departments relating to production and productivity, it has relied on some data supplied by the management and the rest was harvested from the financial data of the company. In process details (in real time) required Time and Motion study and online monitoring, these could not be performed. Similarly, day to day financial details could not be monitored. The ratios and parameters calculated are approximations since the operations are quite complex, for example in some of the Supply Chain estimates.

V Conclusion

The organization is laterally spread as well as vertical, but the vertical span is not large. .

It is noticed that there is less pyramidal structuring and more of a matrix-like structure, (that is to say, lateral and vertical connections in a matrix fashion), although the connections are not shown in the chart, it is quite likely there is a matrix communication network. The building houses all the departments on the same floor, with the executives in glass partitioned office where they can see what is going on. The CEO and executive assistant do not sit in the common area but have separate offices with secretaries screening visitors.

Observation of the office cubicles showed frequent contacts between the members of different departments and passing of paperwork, forms, and contacts through the company emails. There appears to be no internal LAN, all messages and memos are passed on as emails which would add to the Internet data usage and monthly bills.

The use of parameters and ratios can give a barometric picture of the health of the organization further to the analyses provided by accountancy tools in the Balance sheet. It supplements superficial Balance Sheet figures and can diagnose certain problems inherent in the company's style of functioning, such as the accumulation of inventory, EOQ vs JIT systems and other SCM parameters.

The system parameters indicate a return twice a year approximately from a CCD (cash to cycle time) of 156 days. This implies an investment of about 6 months in inventory giving a lead time of 6 months for the various activities relating to procurement, manufacture, and distribution during the 6 months. This clearly shows that reducing the inventory could result in a reduction in lead time in proportion. Additionally, the DSO, DPO, and CCD reflect the credit terms pertaining to the company, offered to customers and effect on total capital requirements. The stated TAKT time and production estimates based on this time indicate overproduction by the factory and consequential piling up of inventory, with loss of incoming cash flow.

Chapter 1

Literature Review

Since the introduction of Scientific Management by Taylor (1), it has been realized that the organization and human resources underlying and fueling it are important in determining the output, productivity and ultimately the profitability of the firm and organization. To this end, increasing the productivity of the organization is ultimately of interest to the management, shareholders, and ultimately the Industry sector and Government in the context of global trade and the National Economy.

A Productive system is defined as the "means by which we transform resource inputs to create useful goods and services as outputs", Buffa & Sarin (2).

Productivity and Efficiency were studied by Gilbreth (3) and others, and subsequent to the end of WWII, developed from quality control work in Japan by Deming and Juran. Japan was found to be very receptive to the QC ideas taught by Deming and Juran, and it is possibly due to the social structure of Japan which pervades their industry. Kolesar(4).

Earlier, Japanese consumer products were known for bad quality whereas, on the other hand, their industry could produce high-quality products for scientific and defense use. After conscientiously following the recommendations of the Juran and Deming teams, the Japanese Industry was able to rise to a pre-eminent position. It is not out of place to state that India is also following in the same path with the emphasis on Six Sigma and ISO standards. Indian consumer industry is also flooded with low-quality consumer goods termed "second" and "third" quality. However, the aerospace, defense, communications and satellite industry is capable of achieving very high standards.

The automated factory now needs to understand and incorporate many other facets of manufacturing besides QC, such as Inventory control, scheduling, PP&C, Materials scheduling, ERP and MRP, Operations scheduling and Human Resource Planning. Some are discussed in Buffa(2), Mahadevan (5), and Eilon (6). Choosing supply chain parameters is often difficult because of the complexities inherent in any industrial system. A number of studies have been performed to identify and quantify supply chain parameters so that objective estimates can be drawn from such measures. SCM came to be found of importance after the implementation of Lean Manufacturing and Japanese JIT concepts. JIT is also known as the Toyota system, apparently having first been implemented at Toyota.

A study by Hoffmann (7), mentioned three metrics of importance:

Demand, Forecast accuracy, Perfect order fulfillment, and Supply Chain cost.

A paper by Anvari et al (8) performed in the Iranian Auto industry compared different parameters using Beamon's model (9) and Gunasekharan's model (10). They find total cash flow time and Cycle time to be important in the Auto industry.

A key paper by Beamon (9) illustrates this and identifies three types of performance measures. Choosing appropriate Supply chain metrics is difficult due to the complexity of most systems. The indicators suggested are resources, output, and flexibility.

In another work by Gunasekharan et al (11) it is pointed out that the role of measures and metrics is important because they influence the tactical, planning, control and operational functions of the organization. Using the results from British companies, certain Framework metrics were emphasized such as order lead time, customer order path and evaluation of supply links.

In the case of capacity utilization, the effectiveness of scheduling techniques was found important. Also for Order Planning metrics, they found that customer query time, product development cycle time and accuracy of forecasting played important roles. Better forecasting was emphasized to remove uncertainties in the supply chain.

Supplier metrics were also mentioned with emphasis on supply delivery performance and supplier lead time. Important Production Metrics were stated to be percentage of defects and Cost per Operation hour along with Capacity Utilization.

An earlier work by Gunasekharan (10), discusses Performance Metrics in a supply chain Environment.

A report by Gamme and Johansson (12), discusses various KPI's (Key Performance Indicators) in the Swedish scenario. A number of KPI's were outlined and it was discovered that as many as 27 new measures could be identified.

Hammesfahn et al (13), state that a fully utilized capacity is the most efficient way to operate a facility, however, the system is then vulnerable to unforeseen uncertainty and change in demand.

In fact, the choice between whether to use JIT or MRP and EOQ is discussed by Abuhilal et al (14). The comparison between JIT and MRP indicates that with a JIT system having continuous ordering these costs increase, compared with the MRP and EOQ system with a Push methodology.

The formula for number of monthly orders is then given by

No. of Monthly orders = [Retailer Forecast – (Retailer Inventory Position – ROP)]/EOQ

Where ROP = reorder point

$$= \mu_d * Lt + Z_{(1-\alpha)} \times \sigma * (Lt)^{0.5}$$

Where μ_d = daily demand

Lt = lead time

$Z_{(1-\alpha)}$ = Factor from Normal distribution for $(1-\alpha)$ service level

And where

$$EOQ = [2*S \, \mu/h]^{0.5}$$

With S= ordering cost, μ average annual demand, h = annual holding cost/unit

Mahadevan (5) derives and mentions several formulae for estimating Supply Chain Performance which are used later in this report.

1.1 JIT and Lean Manufacture.

JIT (Just in Time) derives from the Japanese system originally ascribed to Toyota, where a network of suppliers on call is established and required components can be sourced in minimal time. It requires tuning and once optimized reduces the need for in-house storage of inventory. Implementation is usually not easy due to organizational resistance. In the Japanese setup, it relies on KANBAN cards showing the P (production) and C (Conveyance) status.

INVENTORY CONTROL:

A number of formulae are given in Eilon (6) for different scenarios where the optimal order quantity is estimated:

The Inventory formula for short production periods and small storage charges

$$Q = (2as/I)^{.5}$$

For optimal batch sizes

$$Q = (2as/(I+2B))^{0.5}$$

Several other formulae appear in the literature.

An article by Dooley (15), mentions that the carrying cost for a company is related to the Opportunity cost of holding the inventory item. The appropriate Opportunity cost would then be the Rate of Return or market rate of interest that could be earned if the same money tied up in inventory were invested elsewhere

Use of Nomo graph. The Nomo graph in an analog calculator like a custom made slide rule or a graphical computer which was used before the calculators and computer programs became available. It allows the variation of parameters to get the final function value. It is still found in places where a rough and ready graphical calculation is desired or suitable.

1.2 Determination of the Production Range

A non dimensional ratio p is calculated, where

$P = Y-c/(Ym-c)$ = variable costs/minimum variable costs

After some manipulations the formula obtained by Eilon is

$P = \frac{1}{2}(1/q+q)$, where $q = Q/Qm$

Giving $Q_1 = Qm(p - (p^2-1)^{0.5})$

$Q_2 = Qm(p + (p^2-1)^{0.5})$

This gives the limits of the production range over and below the minimum cost batch size.

The maximum profit batch size is calculable either by algebra or a graphical method.

However, according to Mahadevan (5) using traditional EOQ based inventory control often results in having inventory when not required. MRP should ensure availability of materials at the right place and time, rather than building inventory and cause loss of space and income. The impact of MRP is the reduction of Inventory. Traditional EOQ control maintains a buffer regardless of demand. The other advantage of MRP is to increase transparency and reduce dependence on the Bill of Material (BOM) representation of the products being manufactured.

On the other hand, drawbacks of MRP are:

a) Dependence on data integrity

b) Necessity to update the required databases while changes take place

c) Effect of uncertainties that lie outside the control of personnel (eg Bad Supply Management).

Consequently, the predictions of MRP can be inaccurate, resulting in a reset of the systems on a frequent basis. As a result, several production scheduling changes and effects downstream of the supply chain would occur.

The BULLWHIP effect resulting from the above refers to distortions resulting from changes in demand and ordering patterns at different levels of the supply chain. This has been discussed by Constantino et al (16) where they describe the tradeoff between inventory stability and the Bull whip effect, alternatively called "Demand variability Amplification". According to Burbridge's law, if "**demand is transmitted along a series of inventories using stock control ordering, then each transfer will increase the amplitude of demand variation**". They suggest the use of control charts to regulate the replenishment system.

One way to get some idea of the inherent delay from system parameters is to compute the **Cash to cycle time (CCD)** in days. This is a measure of **SUPPLY CHAIN PERFORMANCE**

The formula used is **CCD= TID +DSO- DPO**

Where TID= Total inventory days= Total investment in Inventory/Annual sales x 365

And DPO = days of payables outstanding = Accounts payable/ value of raw material consumes x 365

With DSO = days of sales outstanding = Accounts receivable/Annual sales x 365

Further parameters to be seen are the Inventory turnover percentage (TO) and number of inventory turns = 1/TO

(Ref Mahadevan (5))

PROJECT PLANNING TOOLS:

In addition to Gantt and PERT/CM, the additional tools that can be used are PDM (procedure diagram method), GERT (Graphical evaluation and review technique), PERT with LOB (Line of Balance).

Traditional control and monitoring mechanisms have included GANTT (bar charts), PERT/CPM (an extension of GANTT charts), Milestone charts and Resource Allocation Methods.

Parallel production lines lead to scheduling problems with loss of production due to slack downtime. A number of studies have been performed, notable being one by Mansoor (17) and Gunther (18)

1.3 Production Planning and Control

A recent paper by Sharma et al (19) describes the salient functions of PP&C. It provides different information to the concerned departments and requires different factors as inputs.

1.4 Organizational Structure

A work by Paterson (20), illustrates the relations between the organizational structure and salary structures. It has been used to establish salary structures at various organizations including the civil services of Rhodesia, Ghana and some private and public firms. Essentially it postulates that remuneration is dependent on the quality of the decisions made by the incumbent at that position or level in the organization. Using a recurrence formula it can be shown that since the decision is dependent on the levels above it that an exponential formula results. Hence, the log of the salary should vary linearly with the hierarchical level.

1.5 Financial Analysis:

The health of the company may be ascertained using certain parameters extracted from the Balance Sheet and other reports.

From the Balance sheet the following ratios can be estimated:

Current Ratio= Current total ASSETS/Current total Liabilities

Cash Ratio = Cash Balance/Current Liability

Quick Ratio = (Cash +Marketable securities+ Accounts receivable)/Current Liabilities

DUPONT IDENTITY

ROE = (Net Profit/Net sales)* (Net Sales/ Avg Total Assets)* (Average T.A/Shareholder Equity)

= Net Profit/ SHE

1.6 SPAN OF CONTROL. According to Graciunas (21), the span of control is dependent on the number of relationships existing between a manager and his/her subordinates, in various combinations (individual and amongst themselves). Accordingly, the number of relationships for a manager with n subordinates is expressed as $n*[2^{(n-1)} + n-1]$

PORTERS 5 Forces Framework:

Since the company is competing internationally, it is necessary to consider the purchasing power of the rupee versus various international currencies, viz. Purchase Power Parity. According to Buffa (1987), "to **compete effectively in a particular international market, we must be at least as productive in the field relative to our own economy as our international competitor is relative to its economy**". Hence productivity improvement takes on an even more important role in corporate strategy.

PESTLE ANALYSIS

The Pestle analysis is an extension of the SWOT analysis. PESTLE consists of

Tools used by marketing analysts to evaluate the changing environment in which the business operates. Hence it is a Tool of Strategic Management.

PESTLE stands for:

POLITICAL, ECONOMIC, SOCIAL, TECHNOLOGICAL LEGAL and ENVIRONMENTAL factors which could affect the business.

In more detail:

- **The political** situation of the country -- how it could affect the industry?
- Prevalent economic factors?
- Effect of culture on the market and its determinants? (**SOCIAL**)
- **Technological** innovations and effect on the market structure?
- **Legislations** and any change in the legislations?
- **Environmental** concerns for the industry? (Cost of Polluting, disposal of waste etc).

Chapter II

FINDINGS

2.1 ORGANIZATIONAL CHART

The organizational structure indicates <u>direct control</u> by the CEO of HR Labour regulations, and planning operations. All other functions are through GMs and DGMs, such as Works, Technical, Marketing, Commercial. At most 4 hierarchical levels exist from GM to the field levels. Within the branches, there is a wide structure with each GM/DGM controlling up to 5 heads at a lateral level. All information from the lower levels goes up through the Managers, then Heads and then GM/DGMs.

The span of control at each hierarchy is at most 5, which is normal.

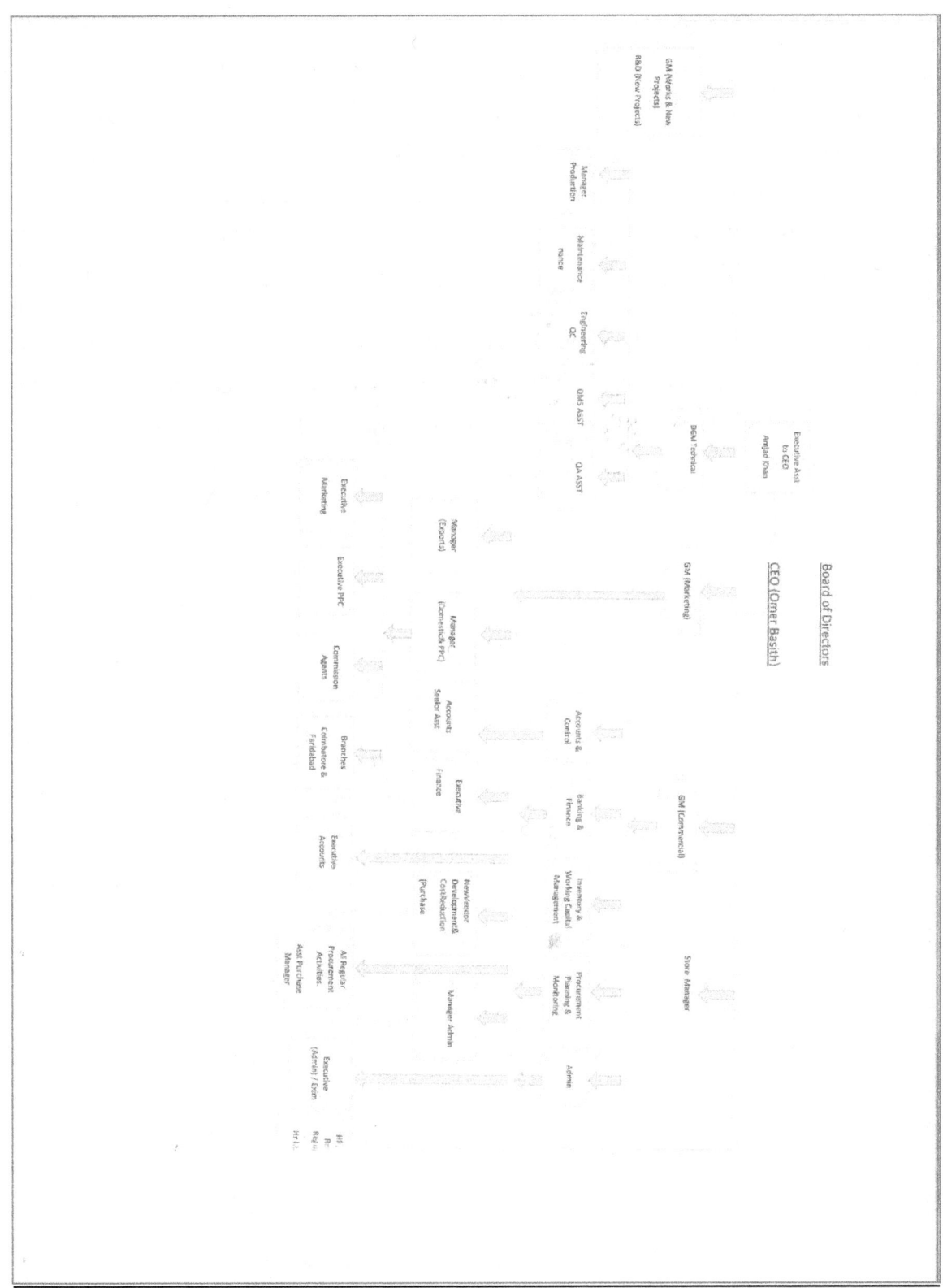

Fig 2.1 Organization Chart

It is noticed that there is less of a pyramid structure and more matrix-like, (that is to say, lateral and vertical connections in a matrix fashion), although the connections are not shown in the chart, it is quite likely there is a matrix communication network. The building houses all the departments on the same floor, with the executives in glass partitioned office where they can see what is going on. The CEO and executive assistant do not sit in the common area but have separate offices with secretaries screening visitors.

Observation of the office cubicles showed frequent contacts between the members of different departments and passing of paperwork, forms, and contacts through the company emails. There appears to be no internal LAN, all messages and memos are passed on as emails which would add to the Internet data usage and monthly bills.

CHAPTER-III

Functioning of Various Departments

3.1 Introduction

In what follows, an overview of the various departments is outlined. Due to the reticence of the management in providing inside details, observations were made personally along with discrete queries to key personnel which gave furtherinferences. Together with the tools of financial and empirical analysis a preliminary picture could be gathered.

Ideally, an organizational culture where superiors and subordinate relations, teamwork and collaboration among different sub units are strong is desired. Overall they should contribute to the organization's health, dynamism and "esprit de corps".

The style of functioning and effectiveness of the organization is not only influenced by the corporate missions and goals, but also certain structural features like the SPAN OF CONTROL. According to Graciunas (21), the span of control is dependent on the number of relationships existing between a manager and his/her subordinates, in various combinations (individual and amongst themselves). Accordingly, the number of relationships for a manager with n subordinates is expressed as $n*[2^{(n-1)} + n-1]$

Lyndall Urwick (22) stressed that the span of control was limited by geographic dispersion and face to face interaction. This view point no doubt was influenced by Urwick's military experience as a colonel in the British Army.

According to the Woodburn Aston studies, Woodward (23), as the evolution of the firm goes from unit operations to mass production and then to process type industry, the span of control changes from 4 to 7 to 10 (median values

As per the current trends with the influence of better communication and Information Technology Revolution, the span of control has increased with a decrease in the number of levels in the organization. Consequently, there could be 20-30 subordinates in a span with at most 5 levels.

TABLE 3.1

Span of Control variables

Kind of Relationship	Variable	Formula
Direct single relationships	a	n
Cross relationships	b	$n(n-1)$
Direct group relationships	c	$n(2^n/2 - 1)$
Total direct single and cross relationships (a + b)	d	n^2
Total direct single and group (a + c)	e	$n(2^n/2)$
Total direct and cross relationships (a + b + c)	f	$n(2^n/2 + n - 1)$

Current trends appear to be an increase in the span of control with a decrease in the number of levels in the organization. This is a consequence of the Information revolution. As such many IT firms have flat structures with fewer vertical levels.

3.2 ACCOUNTING AND FINANCE FUNCTION

STRUCTURE OF FINANCE FUNCTION

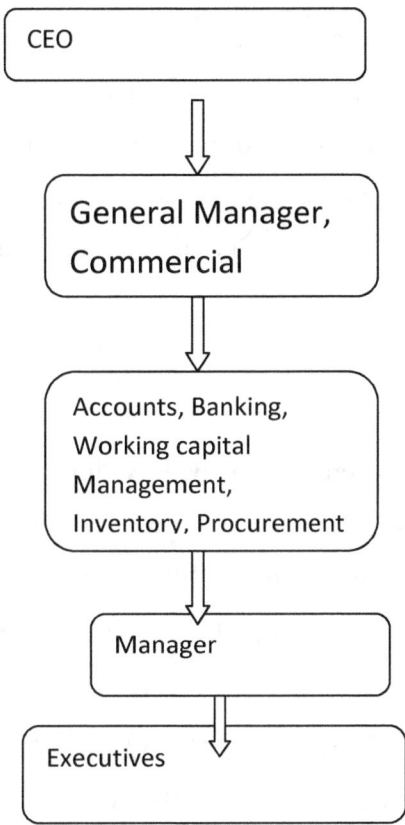

Fig 3.2.1 Finance authority flow

WORKING CAPITAL MANAGEMENT

Working capital management is concerned with current assets and current liabilities and the relationship that exists between them. The term "current assets" refers to those assets, which in the ordinary course of business can be or will be converted into cash within one year without undergoing a diminution in value and without disruption of operation. The goal of working capital management is to manage the firm's current assets and liabilities in such a way a satisfactory that level of working capital is maintained. The company has availed working capital from the nationalized Banks in the form of over draft accounts and from the Directors.

TRADE CREDIT

Trade credit refers to the credit extended by the suppliers of goods and services in the normal course of transaction/business/ sale of the firm according to trade practices; cash is not paid immediately for purchases but after an agreed period of time. In case of SSS Pvt. Ltd credit the suppliers allow period with in 30days.

ACCOUNTS RECEIVABLE/ RECEIVABLE MANAGEMENT

The term receivable is defined as the debt owed by customers arising from the sale of goods or services in the ordinary course of business when the firm makes an ordinary sale of goods or services and does not receive payment. The firm grants trade credit and creates accounts receivable, which could be collected in future.

TYPES OF SOFTWARE FOR ACCOUNTING PROCEDURE

The company uses <u>SAP</u> software under license which handles ERP functions. Monthly visits are arranged with SAP representatives who perform the software upkeep. In addition, Tally software which covers all recently updated accounting standards and also covers VAT concept which makes it very easy for the company to fill the tax according to rules and regulation. GST is currently being implemented. A separate department exists in the organization with consultants coming in regularly to do the reports with SAP and ERP software.

Excel software is used for day to day activities involving internal reports and tabulations.

ACCOUNTING POLICIES OF SOLID STATE SYSTEMS

1. FIXED ASSETS

Fixed assets are stated at cost of acquisition less depreciation, except land at Hoskote, which is shown at revalued cost.

2. DEPRECIATION

Depreciation on fixed assets has been calculated on the straight-line method at the rates specified in schedule XIV of the Companies Act 1956

3. INVENTORIES

Raw materials & work in process are valued at cost. Finished goods are valued at cost or net realizable value whichever is less

4. **INVESTMENT**

Investment is valued at cost.

5. BENEFITS

All employees, whether casual or permanent, are covered under ESI from day one. ESI and PF are covered when the employees get into the system. Overtime is fixed as per policies. Gratuity is allowed after Five years of service.

6. BORROWING COSTS

Borrowing cost including interest and other expenses for the specific borrowing of funds that are attributing to the acquisition, construction and fabrication of fixed assets are capitalized till they are put to use.

7. GENERAL

Accounting policies not specifically referred conform to the general accounting practices and are certified by the CPA's in their annual report.

3.3 PRODUCTION FUNCTION

STRUCTURE OF PRODUCTION

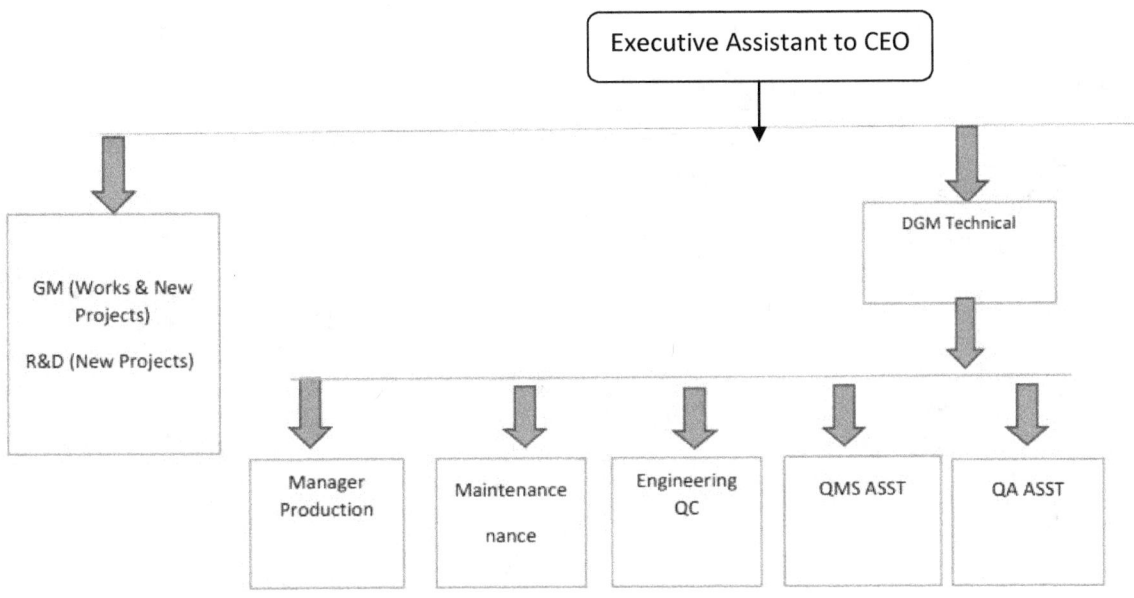

Figure 3.3.1 Production department

Under Head of Production the structure is as shown:

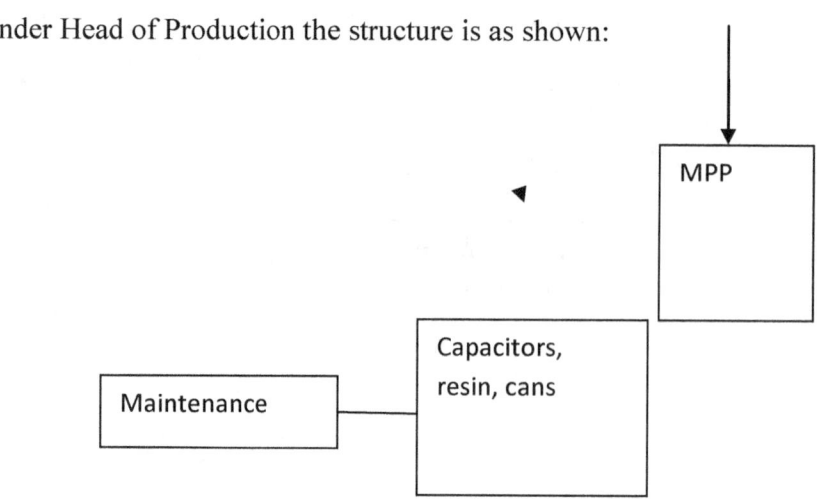

Figure 3.3.2 Structure below Production Head

Every category is centrally planned. ERP is under a separated department which covers all material planning and resource planning, using standard software like SAP. Raw materials are indented and given to the purchase department.

The purchase dept, material dept., and production dept. discuss with general manager technical who takes a decision about the procurement. Materials are sourced as per the requirements and projections of software. In addition, safety stock is maintained to tide over fluctuations and demands from customers of special status (preferred customers). Production on any order is stopped to accommodate the orders of preferred customers. This leads to delays in the ongoing job together with labour time, storage of unfinished components and similar associated problems.

3.4 PROJECT PLANNING TOOLS:

In addition to Gantt and PERT/CM, the additional tools that can be used are PDM (procedure diagram method), GERT (Graphical evaluation and review technique), PERT with LOB (Line of Balance).

Traditional control and monitoring mechanisms have included GANTT (bar charts), PERT/CPM (an extension of GANTT charts), Milestone charts and Resource Allocation Methods.

Parallel production lines lead to scheduling problems with loss of production due to slack down time. A number of studies have been performed, notable being one by Mansoor (17), and Gunther (18).

It was noticed at SSS that production is kept to 20,000 pcs per day per machine for normal jobs, however when a priority of regular customer's job entered the system, the production lines were stopped and the preferred customer's job put on line.

The advantage of Line Balancing is that an even distribution of work occurs across stations.

Thus it is possible to have parallel lines with LOB programs such that an even distribution of work occurs across stations, Dar El Mansoor (17). An extract of Dar el's assignment rules for work stations is illustrated in Buffa (2).

To summarize, the rules are:

a) Select lowest cycle time corresponding to work stations

b) Select the task with highest weight/priority

c) Select next highest task

Continue till remaining unassigned time is less than or equal to the slack units available

d) Work backward

e) Repeat with cycle time having one more unit and continue

3.5 PP&C (Production Planning and Control)

In the traditional set up the PP&C functions may be illustrated by the following schematic

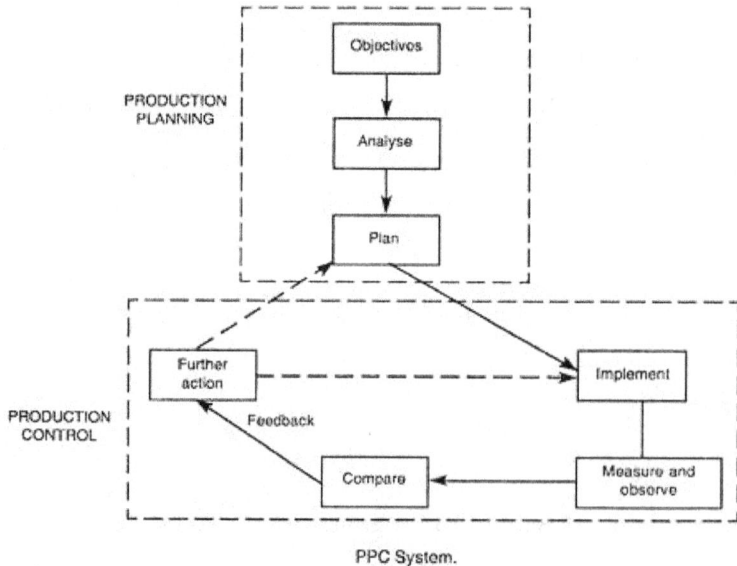

PPC System.

Figure 3.5.1 PPC system

Data was maintained on cards and activities plotted on Gantt and Pert Charts. Inventory, Material, scheduling and other activities were the purview of the PP&C group. This involved Job cards, Job orders, route cards and associated paper work. This has been taken over by computerized systems today. After receipt of an order a form or card was prepared:

Order No... No. of Products	Date handed over to works	Date fixed for Delivery	Design No.....
Operations..			
Special Instructions...			
Quantity of material requisitioned		Specification of material requisitioned	
Work commenced		Order issued by	
Date completed..............		Finally tested by	

Figure 3.5.2 Example of Job Card

Subsequently, various subsidiary cards and forms had to be prepared.

Example of the various cards traditionally used:

JOB ORDER

Job No.					Work Order No.	
Workers No.	Name of operation,	Rate	Amount	Day	Timings	
		Rs. P.				
						off on off on off on off on
		Total	Signature of Foreman			

Figure 3.5.3 Example of Job Order card

Next Job cards had to be prepared for various operations

Work Order No............							Date ....
Job No............................							Man's Rate ....
Name of Operator...........							Time allowed ....

Job	Operations	Material No.	Date	Time		Time taken	No. of products
				Started at	Finished at		

Total time taken ......

Labour Cost ....

(Foreman)

Figure 3.5.4 Sample of Job Card

The flow of material on the various jobs had to be decided by a routing card

ROUTE CARD

Part No........	Symbol........	Lot size	Drawing No..........·			

Operation No.	Shop	Machine	Jigs and Fixtures required	Set-up Time	Time reqd. per lot	Labour rate
1.						
2.						
3.						
4.						
5.						
6.						
7.						

Figure 3.5.5 Route Card

Consequently, the PP&C department needed the following information:

1. Materials requirement

2. Availability of materials

3. Output capacity of production machines

4. Sequence of operations

5. Operation time for each operation

6. Material handling services

7. Progress of work accomplishment.

All these have now been replaced with online forms and tracking possible with software with database management.

3.5.1 MATERIAL DEPARMENT & STORES DEPARTMENT

Material department in Solid State Systems holds a special significance because of various categories of products and models which are used in the production process.

In particular, the basic raw material which is metalized poly film is manufactured by vacuum spray deposition in-house, rather than sourced from other quarters. The material department discusses with other sections in the production dept and according to the requirements and production stage, a decision is made to procure material. Stores department has separate storerooms in which materials, finished goods are stored and also storerooms are designed in such a way that raw material can be used easily.

3.6 RESEARCH AND MANAGEMENT

Minimal R&D is performed; as it is felt the technology has reached an optimum level for the requirements. The technology was developed over several years, with induction of personnel from their key competitors who have brought in their know-how from the competitors.

Motivation is performed through incentives to reach and achieve standard goals.

The performance is evaluated every day with the chart, including the standard production rate and actual production rate.

3.7 MARKETING DEPARTMENT

STRUCTURE OF MARKETING DEPARTMENT

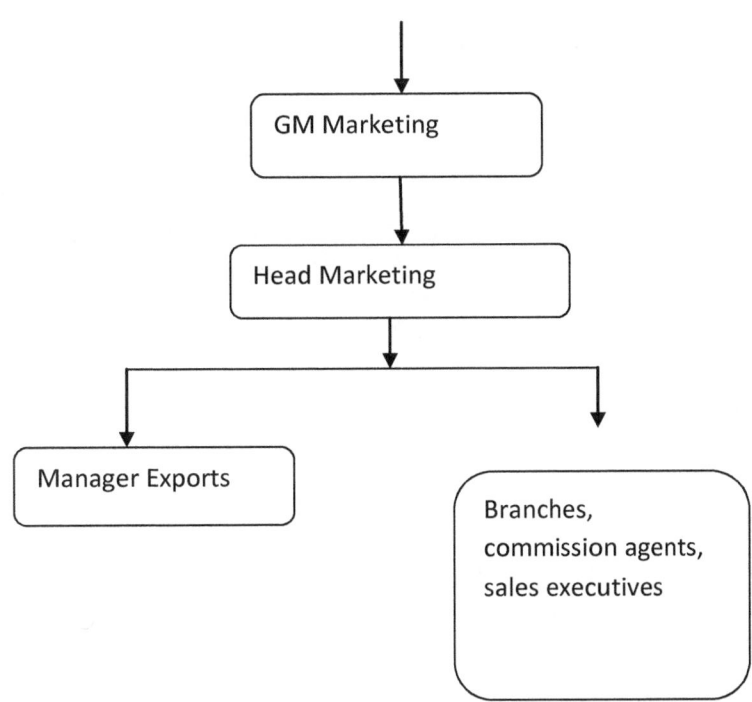

Figure 3.7.1

There is no separate centralized marketing department as such. The HQ supplies finished goods to the distribution centers, which then supply to dealers and direct to customers. The Software enables the HQ to coordinate centrally using ERP and SAP. Direct control is possible in this way through the CEO and his assistant, bypassing intermediary levels.

3.8 HUMAN RESOURCE FUNCTION

ADMINISTRATION

The administration activities are as follows:

Recruitment

The main sources of recruitment are

Open advertisement

Management trainees

Campus selection

Vacancies to be filled by recruitment in a department will be notified to the personnel department in employment requisition form, on respect of which personnel department will take steps for recruitment of personnel after obtaining approval if any from the competent authorities. Graduates from the commerce and accounting streams are recruited for office jobs. The admin clerks are required to have computer proficiency. At the GM level and above recruitment is also through experience.

Interview and selection

The personnel department in consultation with the head of the departments concerned scrutinizes application received in response to advertisements and list of candidates to be called for interview will be drawn up.

The human resource development manager will constitute the selection committee. Once the candidate is selected he as to go through a performance test after six months.

Wages and salary administration.

The salary for the employee is given according to their qualification, designation, and experience. They are being given an annual increment every year. Almost 65% of the salary to employees is given through the bank.

Job categorization according to work duties:

Group A- general manager

Group B-manager

Group C- section in charge.

Group D- Operators/workers.

Grievance

Grievance means a complaint of an individual workman in regard to payment, wages, overtime, leave, transfer, promotion, seniority, work assignments, working condition, designation, and non extension of any welfare, amenity or benefit due shall be dealt by human resource development department.

Settlements regarding Retirement, Death etc: Settlement such as provident fund, gratuity, leave etc on the date of retirement, resignation, death, termination and voluntary retirement will be dealt in this section.

Gratuity for the service rendered by the employee according to the Gratuity Act is 15 days salary for every completed year of services. Gratuity eligibility becomes available after 5 years of service. The entire employees who come under provident fund Act must contribute minimum 12%. The employee should at least a minimum period of 5years in the organization after which he/she becomes eligible, for benefits of provident fund. Regardless of service length, all employees are enrolled under ESI from the first day.

WELFARE MEASURES

Consistent with the policy of the company through its employee and their families happy and contended, it is operating a number of schemes to promote their welfare.

Employee welfare fund scheme.

A fee of 2% is given to the children of employees. Other facilities like medical and transport facility are provided.

Canteen facilities:

The canteen facility is on a contract basis. Food, coffee, tea, and snacks are served in a separate area.

Transport facilities:

Bus facility for up to 60 persons till Krishnarajapuram is provided; others use private vehicles and stay in the local area.

Safety equipment:

Employees are required to wear hand gloves, safety boots etc to ensure complete safety from risks involved arising out of accidents during factory duties.

MOTIVATION

Apart from rewards and pecuniary benefits, the main driving force to fuel the worker in the organization is the Motivation factor. The traditional theories of McGregor (X-Y), Maslow, Herzberg, McLelland, Adams, Vroom, Skinner and the Porter Lawlor extensions are well known. These are given credence in the western economies where human beings are viewed as Assets. However, this attitude has yet to take effect in the majority of medium-sized Indian businesses, the exceptions being the Multinationals and the small micro businesses where personal relations are viewed as important tools.

In the Indian context, the main motivators at the factory level appear to be the Hygiene and motivation (2 factor) and 3-factor models. A subsistence level of pay enabling the worker to manage the household and day to day expenses is barely the minimum, with additional bonuses and incentives doing the rest.

Since the majority of the work force is temporary, the management does not see the need to extend additional incentives to achieve higher production, furthermore due to the nature of the automated manufacturing process; additional incentives may not yield any further additional gains. This viewpoint and practice leads, however, to additional training and learning time for the new recruits to attain the competence level for efficient production. In the long run, it would account for lost time and wastage of material which would negate any financial gain made by hiring and firing temporary staff merely to avoid paying of benefits.

Suffice it to say that the extra amount of work got from the individual depends on the organization and the style of management. In the words of General Slim of Burma **"Leadership is the mixture of persuasion, compulsion, and example, that makes men do what you want them to do"** Barney Frank said it more subtly: **"The great leader is the one who can show people that their self-interest is different from that which they perceived"** @

@ Babcock and Morse (24), p 148

PERFORMANCE APPRAISAL:

A performance appraisal system is a strong tool in the development of human resources in the organization. It is considered as mutual feedback to the management and thereby helps to define career growth, training needs and other human resource development interventions required for aiding self-development.

Performance is the key index for the individual and for the company as a whole. It is therefore vitally important that every individual has a clear understanding of his or her work, objectives and responsibilities because performance will measure against these..

Performance management must create a shared vision of purpose and aims of the organization. It must help each individual to understand and recognize their part of the contribution to the organization's success and thereby managing and improving the performance of the both individual and organization. High performance by way of performance management is the only guarantee for survival in an unpredictable and dynamic world. Managers have to continuously motivate their employees besides considering other factors that enable superior levels of performance. Rewards are commensurate with level in the hierarchy (Figs 3.4.1-3.4.2), consistent with the Decision Band theory propounded by Paterson (20).

Infrastructure:

It is the responsibility of the department heads to identify, define, provide and maintain appropriate work facilities that are required for the performance of activities, processes and service in order to ensure conformance and specified requirements. Facilities include adequate workspace and associated utilities, equipment, hardware and software, suitable maintenance and other necessary supporting services. To achieve the performance of activities, processes, end products, delivery and service to the customer's satisfaction the necessary quality plans, work instructions, drawings, test procedures and checklist are prepared and adopted.

Work Environment

Management recognizes that the most valuable asset is its people. Therefore, the management and head of departments consider the work environment as corporate criteria and endeavors to provide its employees with a conducive work environment. This criterion of work environment includes regulation and statutory requirements such as safety and health, ambient working condition etc., and SSPL considers the above as the minimum requirements of all departments.

OPERATING PROCEDURE OF TRAINING IN SOLID STATE SYSTEMS

Aims of the training program are

- To establish procedures for providing training to personnel and customers.
- To give suitable knowledge to the employees, especially casual and temporary employees hired on contract basis

Total number of employees in SSS

Approximately 230 employees are working at the main plant, on both day and night shifts including factory workers and casual factory workers. Included in this are executive employees, engineers, and department heads, and also managers. Previously it was 350 employees. All temps are given training for one month.

At the time of study due to down time about 50% of the work force was on standby at a reduced salary.

Training program: Minimal In-house training is provided to the temps and they are supposed to function efficiently during their tenure. The temps are replaced every six months or as needed. **It is difficult to expect top quality from such practices, however the management claim that the automatic machines detect inherent defects automatically,**

The Human Resource Department aims at helping people to acquire competencies required for the performance of functions. The advancement of human resources is possible through education, training and sharing experience.

Human resource development departments are also better known as personnel departments. In most organizations, the HRD functions are done by the personnel department. The main functions of the personnel department are:

Administration: The staff details are maintained in a data base with EXCEL sheets. Salaries and increments are decided periodically as well as hiring and retrenchment of workers depending on the order positions. A large number of casual workers are kept on the roster, with only essential trained staff retained to man the metallizers and slitting machines. All decisions are made with final approval of the HR team, Assistant to CEO and CEO in closed meetings. Position of materials, orders, dispatches and cash are entered into the SAP and EXCEL data bases weekly.

Welfare measures: Employees are enrolled in ESI and given health benefits immediately on joining. Gratuity eligibility accrues after 5 years of service. Employees eligible for Provident Fund membership must contribute 12% minimum of their salaries.

Good industrial relations. Employees are provided transport to Krishnarajapuram from where they can take buses and train onwards to the city. Snacks and food are available in the canteen on contract basis. Safety equipment is supplied to the employees.

Chapter IV

PRODUCTION & QC

The Production in Solid State Systems is wholly in-house, starting from metallization of the polyester film used in the capacitors, to the finished products.

Production Planning and Control is regardable as the nervous system of the organization, Sharma (19). The optimum and efficient utilization of resources, men, time and machinery is dependent on PP&C.

4.1 Receipt of Orders

The process of receipt and further processing can best be described pictorially. A flow chart of the PPC functions from Start to Finish is given below

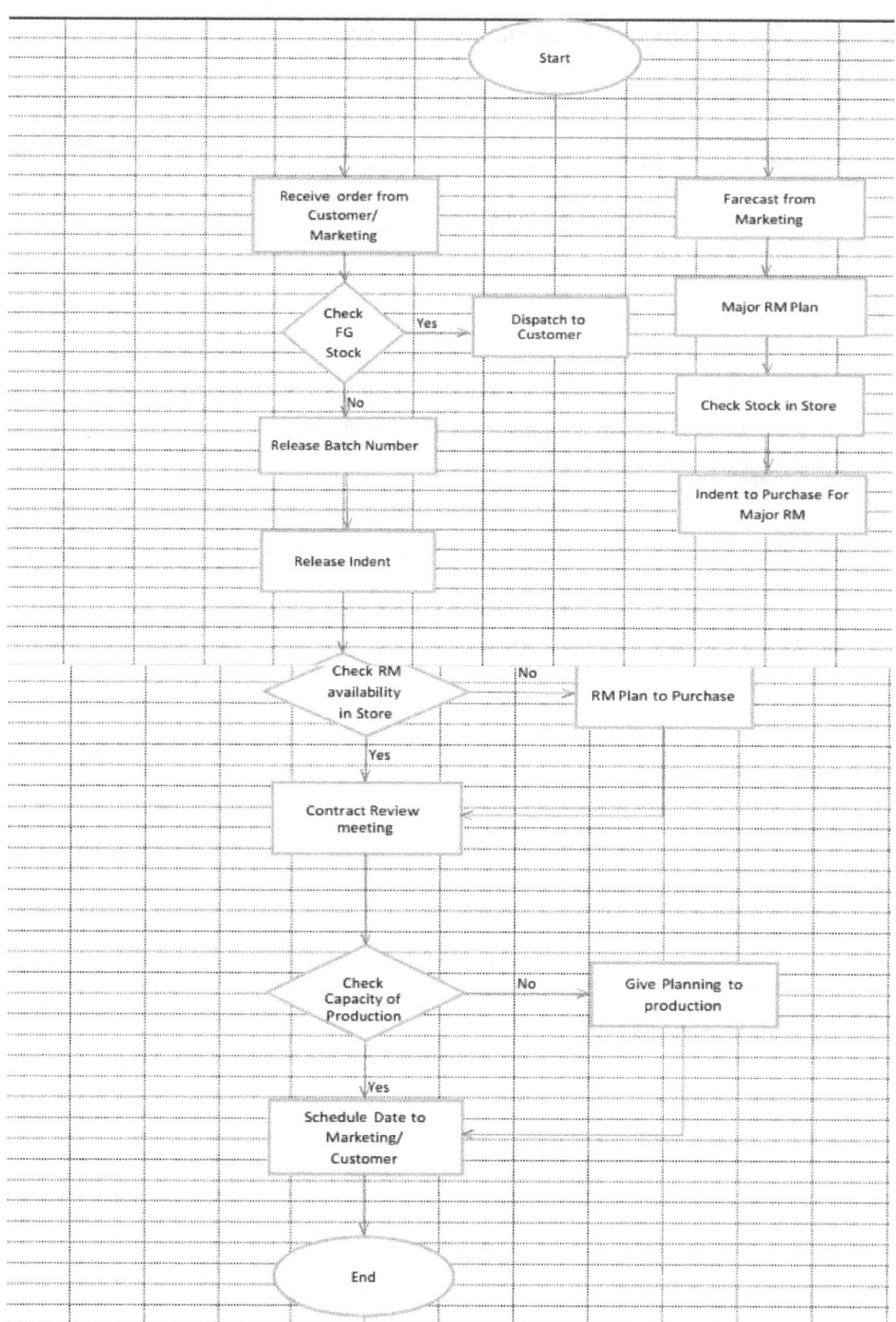

Figure 4.1.1: Flow Chart

The data from orders are filled out in a form having date required for delivery, batch number and estimate for raw materials. The list of raw material is sent to the stores, and then the Stores department informs the availability of materials. Periodic stocks reviews are held and shared with Production Marketing and PPC sections.

The scheduling of machines is done by the Production department. Jobs are loaded by the priority given during scheduling. Urgent jobs are sent to the top of the queue. If there are more than 20000 pieces in the job, it is postponed to the next day.

Marketing Department forecasts are used to coordinate depending on the lead times for the job.

The demand for particular components depends on the time of year. For instance, demand for AC's is higher during the summer, so production of components is enhanced during November to July. Similarly, demand for Washing Machines is high from July to September in the summer months. Demand for pumps follows that of ACs. The replacement of fluorescent and ballast tube lights by LED lights has decreased demand for associated components.

After the enquiry from customers, the SAP software is used to generate a bill of materials and a costing estimate. The average lead time required to start the job is 10 to 15 days.

SAP database is updated daily and indents are updated twice a week for procurement. Certain components like aluminum cans are made in-house at an offsite facility, whereas plastic cans are procured from outside.

Metallization of the polyester film starts with slitting the film obtained in large rolls. Normally after metallization, these are then split into 4 subdivisions lengthwise. These are then rolled onto bobbins for further use. A part of this product is kept aside for sale to other companies. About 1-2 tons a day are produced. Time for the entire process from the start of winding to finish is about 4 days, with a **takt** time of 0.6 seconds per piece (total time/total number of pieces) Mahadevan (5). The lead time for the batch is stated as 4 days.

The resin is made in-house and aluminum cans also made in-house at ancillary facilities near the main factory.

Two metallization units were procured from China 10 years ago; these cause the largest bottle necks in the entire process due to breakdowns. The Chinese spraying units have an MTBF of 300 hours or 15 days. Hence one can expect breakdowns once to twice a month (MTBF= mean time between failures). Another bottleneck occurs in the winding of film onto bobbins to make the capacitors.

The maximum output capacity at present is 35000 to 38000 pieces per day (at 24-hour level). However, the main production lines for unit batch manufacture are restricted to 20000 pieces per day.

Quality control: Automatic Quality checks are performed on each piece by applying 2X rated voltage for 2 seconds, termed breakdown voltage test.

Checks are also performed on the metalized bobbins by testing the starting 1-meter piece on a voltage machine to determine the resistance.

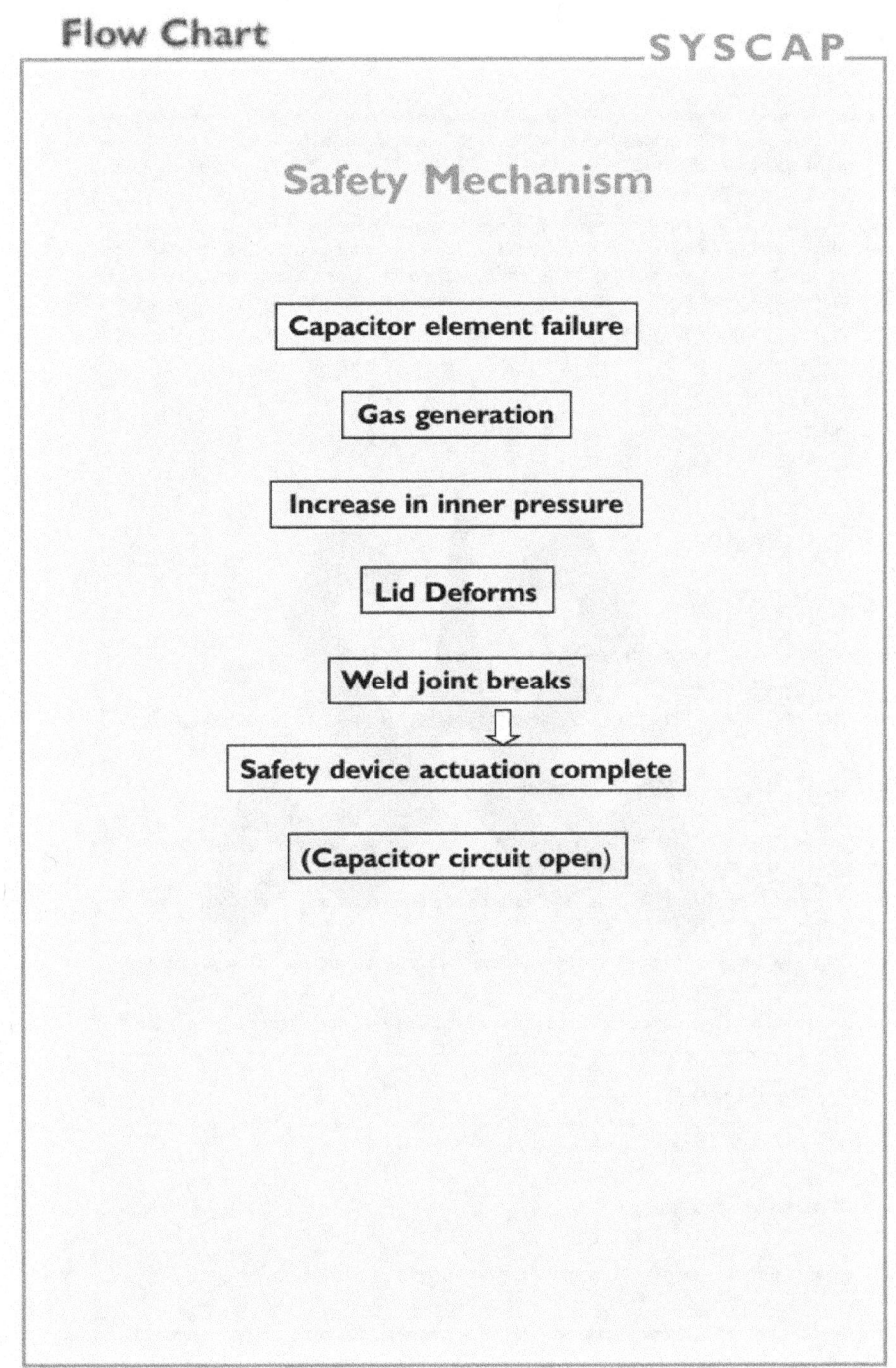

Figure 4.1.2 Built-in quality –failure check

The Process

Syscap capacitors are manufactured using superior quality Metallised Polypropylene (MPP) film on state-of-the-art winding machines. The MPP film has an alloy of Zn & Al vapour deposited on one side with a free margin on one of the edges. The film varies in thickness in the range of 5 to 10 Microns depending on the application voltage and operating conditions.

The capacitor elements are wound on High Precision Automatic Winding Machines in controlled conditions of temperature and humidity. The wound elements are then sprayed on both ends with a metal (Zn) to make an electrical contact with the electrodes. This serves as a connection for the two terminations. The sprayed elements with connecting leads are assembled into a metal or plastic container and encapsulated with a polyurethane resin.

All the capacitors are subjected to 100% electrical testing for all routine tests viz.,

Visual
- Finishing and Marking

Mechanical
- Dimensions

Electrical
- Capacitance
- Tan delta
- High voltage electrical withstand test between terminals and container
- Insulation resistance between terminals and container

SYSCAP CAPACITORS DO NOT CONTAIN ANY ENVIRONMENTALLY HAZARDOUS MATERIALS.

The Quality Assurance System

A quality assurance system employing statistical tools is implemented at three stages during the manufacturing process to ensure control & to continuously monitor the quality of the capacitors.

Data is collected at the SPC gateways which is used to generate reports on the control features of the manufacturing process using "Statistical Process Control" software.

Type Tests are continually being carried out in the In-house test facility as per International standards & also as per customer specifications & requests.

Quality is monitored on a continual basis to ensure production of highly reliable capacitors.

Quality Checks

Quality Checks are carried out at the following stages :-
- Raw Material Stage
- Work in Process(Manufacturing Activity)
- Finished goods

Capacitors are tested 100 % at semi-finished and finished stages to ensure complete conformance to critical parameters.

Process conformance is ensured by continuous monitoring of key equipment & process parameters as well as checks on In-process components.

Apart from the above routine tests, regular type tests are conducted to ensure that the capacitors meet performance, life and safety requirements.

Figure 4.1.3 QA System

Apart from the individual tests done automatically by the machines, there are little or no Quality checks during production, or on the finished products. It is claimed that of a total of 8 lakh units made per month, there is wastage of 4000 pieces and .3 to .5% rejections per month. The quality aimed at is stated to be 95% acceptance by the customers. Since the quality obtained by the automated functions of the batch machines are satisfactory, the manual checks are kept to a minimum.

Figure 4.1.4 Metallization unit

Figure 4.1.5   Winding unit

4.2 JIT and Lean Manufacture.

At the time of the study, Solid State Systems had a large unsold inventory taking up almost half the ground floor. It was claimed that due to GST implementation, orders had slackened, the buffer inventory was stated as 8 days, and residual raw material could provide for one month's production. Finished goods could provide for 15-20 days normal orders.

The orders constitute a Pull model, supplied through buffer stocks, while the factory pushes stocks into the various sites and go-downs.

Supplies from the city take 1 day, within Karnataka 3 days, from the rest of the country 7 days, and from abroad 1 to 1.5 months.

Storage at other factory locations is used to provide for orders nearby, and about 10 days stock was stored at of site locations and distribution centers. Supply is done through road transport.

It is claimed the entire technology is indigenous. The manufacture of the metallized poly film is also a main objective as it is also sold separately to other manufacturers for various purposes.

4.3 INVENTORY CONTROL:

The calculations of EOQ and reorder point were not available; the method used is to use heuristics of keeping a buffer of 8 days stock at the factory. Finished stock is stored for up to one month. As such a large stock of un- shipped product is stored in the warehouse on the ground floor, occupying a large area.

Stock is also kept for valued customers with a track record so that immediate supplies can be made when and as required without delay.

A number of formulae are given in Eilon (6) for different scenarios where the optimal order quantity is estimated:

The Inventory formula for short production periods and small storage charges

$Q = (2as/I)^{.5}$

For optimal batch sizes

$Q = (2as/(I+2B))^{0.5}$

Several other formulae appear in the literature.

Use of Nomo graph. The Nomo graph in an analog calculator like a custom made slide rule or a graphical computer which was used before the calculators and computer programs became available. It allows the variation of parameters to get the final function value. It is still found in places where a rough and ready graphical calculation is desired or suitable.

4.4 Determination of the Production Range Limits

A non dimensional ratio p is calculated, where

$P = Y-c/(Y_m-c) = $ variable costs/minimum variable costs

After some manipulations the formula obtained by Eilon(6) is

$P = \frac{1}{2}(1/q+q)$, where $q = Q/Q_m$

Giving $Q_1 = Q_m(p - (p^2-1)^{0.5})$

$Q_2 = Q_m(p + (p^2-1)^{0.5})$

This gives the limits of the production range over and below the minimum cost batch size.

The maximum profit batch size is calculable either by algebra or a graphical method.

However, according to Mahadevan (5), using traditional EOQ based inventory control often results in having inventory when not required. MRP should ensure availability of materials at the right place and time, rather than building inventory and cause loss of space and income. The impact of MRP is the reduction of Inventory. Traditional EOQ control maintains a buffer regardless of demand. The other advantage of MRP is to increase transparency and reduce dependence on the Bill of Material (BOM) representation of the products being manufactured.

On the other hand, drawbacks of MRP are:

a) Dependence on data integrity

b) Necessity to update the required databases while changes take place

c) Effect of uncertainties that lie outside the control of personnel (eg Bad Supply Management).

Consequently, the predictions of MRP can be inaccurate, resulting in a reset of the systems on a frequent basis. As a result, several production scheduling changes and effects downstream of the supply chain would occur.

The BULLWHIP effect resulting from the above refers to distortions resulting from changes in demand and ordering patterns at different levels of the supply chain. This may also be related to small span of control with more vertical levels, Ouchi (25)

One way to get some idea of the inherent delay from system parameters is to compute the **Cash to cycle time (CCD)** in days. This is a measure of profitability and liquidity in terms of cash availability.

4.4.1 SUPPLY CHAIN PERFORMANCE.

Supply chain processes	Performance measures	Performance Dimensions						
		Cost	Quality	Time	Productivity	Flexibility	Reliability	Customer service
Plan	Forecast accuracy		*				*	
	Degree of Information sharing		*				*	*
	Product development cycle time			*				
	Total cycle time			*	*			
	Product variety					*		*
	Information carrying cost	*						
	Number of order changes		*				*	
	ROI	*			*			
	Degree of buyer supplier partnership		*			*	*	
	Number of changes in product schedule		*				*	
	Number of plans that meets schedules		*				*	

Fig 4.4.1 Some parameters of impact on SCM

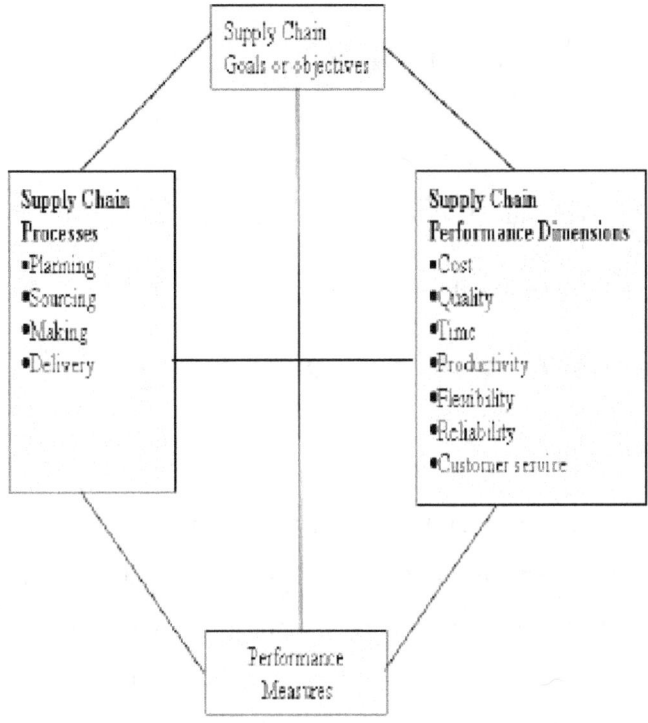

Performance Dimensions of an Activity or Process.

Fig 4.4.2

The formula used is **CCD= TID +DSO- DPO**

Where TID= Total inventory days= Total investment in Inventory/Annual sales x 365

And DPO = days of payables outstanding = Accounts payable/ value of raw material consumes x 365

With DSO = days of sales outstanding = Accounts receivable/Annual sales x 365

Further parameters to be seen are the Inventory turnover percentage (TO) and number of inventory turns = 1/TO

From the Balance sheet seen in the appendix for 2015, the parameters may be estimated as follows:

Material consumed to finished goods = Total Inventory/Annual sales= 19/24x 365= .8215

TID=, 8215x 365= 300

DPO= Accounts payable/value of Ram materials consumed = 7.16/11.45x365= 228

DSO = A/C receivable/Annual sales= 7.45/32.55 x 365 = 83.5

Hence CCD= TID + DS-DPO= 300 +83.5-228 = 156

The system parameters indicate a return twice a year approximately from a CCD (cash to cycle time) of 156 days. This implies an investment of about 6 months in inventory giving a lead time of 6 months for the various activities relating to procurement, manufacture, and distribution during the 6 months. This clearly shows that reducing the inventory could result in a reduction in lead time in proportion. Additionally, the DSO, DPO, and CCD reflect the credit terms pertaining to the company, offered to customers and effect on total capital requirements.

The inventory ratio and the number of inventory turns are TO and TN, given by 82.15% and 1.21 which are the traditional measures of supply chain performance.

Taking the **takt** time of 0.6 seconds (i.e. 0.6 seconds to produce one item), in 156 days, assuming 24X7 operations, a total of 156*24*3600/0.6 pcs are produced. This calculates to 2 2344000 pcs. On the average, a daily output of 144000 pcs is produced. Since the stated production is a maximum of 38000 pcs per day this implies over production of 144000/38000 times or about 3.8 times.

This calculation illustrates that the factory **has been overproducing**, probably in anticipation of seasonal orders and orders from preferred customers where ready shipment could be made from stock.

4.5 Analysis

It is known that there are bottle necks in the process caused by mechanical problems especially at the sputtering machines (Metallizers). No doubt, due to this, overproduction is attempted to tide over such breakdowns.

The solution for such a situation could include

A) DECOUPLING OF PRODUCTION LINES

The chain and production line can be decoupled at certain points, where the material is fed in separately but not continuously, Mahadevan (5). The decoupling is done in the inventory in separate stages. This obviates the need for close monitoring of the supply chain. Thus each stage can be separately decentralized with relatively higher levels of independence. As a result, decentralized Planning and Control with separate units occurs.

B) SEPARATE STAGES AT BOTTLENECKS

The problem may be alleviated by having better maintenance of the problem machines and/or including them in separate stages where continuous supply is not an essential feature of the process. Further application of Decoupling could be advantageous here.

C) INCORPORATE LEAN MANUFACTURE and JIT

The software used is capable of handling this feature; however, it is at present being used merely to compile tables for manual reporting.

At the time of the study, the orders were not coming in due to the new implementation of GST. A number of staff had been laid off due to the slack production. These staff were under contract through an agency who continually supply temps and casual workers, with minimum 10th standard Matric qualification.

4.6 PRODUCT PROFILE

APPLICATIONS:

a) Power factor capacitors from 2 Mfd to 150 Mfd.

b) Fixed power factor correction for motors, transformers, pumps, refrigerators, washing machines etc.

Features:

- Special p.v.c film with heavy edge metallization on both the sides for better electrical contact.
- Capacitors in cylindrical shaped metal enclosures mechanically well suited for 'stand alone' installations.
- Heavy edge metallization to ensure high inrush current withstand capability up to 400X in.
- Continuous working temperature - up to 80 degree C.
- Resin impregnated capacitor.
- Suitable for flexi-banking.

Safety:

Self-healing

Discharge resistors

Pressure sensitive disconnectors (cutoffs)

Available in non-polluting, non PCB, bio-degradable.

Applications

- Power Factor Correction in Low Voltage network
- Fixed power factor correction
- Harmonic filters
- Starting capacitors for fans and pumps
- Capacitors for washing machines
- Refrigerators, freezers, and cold storage display units

Features

Capacitors in cylindrical shapes within built indicator coil

Heavy edge metallization/wave cut edge to ensure high inrush current and with stand capability.

Special resistivity and profile of metallization for enhanced life, suitable

for flexible banking

Fig 4.6.1 Representative product range

- Self-healing and pressure sensitive disconnectors (inbuilt)
- Non-PCB, PU resin filled
- Protective steel enclosure and discharge resistor.

2. APP (20F)

Application

- PF correction in LV network
- Fixed power factor correction
- APFC systems
- Harmonic filters

Features

- Bi-axially oriented hazy to ensure good oil impregnation.
- Suitable for flexi banking
- High inrush current with stand capability
- Especially vacuum processed, oil impregnated design.

Safety

- Internal fuse design
- Non-polluting and non-PCB oil.
- Protective steel enclosure and discharge resistor.

Application

Fixed power factor correction, motors, and transformers.

APFC system and harmonic filters.

Features

- Best suited for APFC due to compact space saving design unique finger proof termination
- Heavy edge metallization/wave cute edge to ensure high inrush current with stand capability up to 250Xin
- Special resistivity and profile of metallization for enhanced life.

Safety

- Self- healing
- Discharge resistors and pressure sensitive disconnector

- Available in non-polluting, non SF6 inert gas.

Standard Duty Capacitors

Suitable for application in…

- Fixed power factor correction e.g. transformer/motor compensation
- Automatic power factor correction systems
- Harmonic filters
- Special design to allow banking of several units in cases where large compensation is required.
- Available in single phase design for special applications
- Inrush current withstand capability - 200 x I_n
- Finger proof CLAMPTITE terminals to reduce risk of accidental contact & to ensure firm termination in cylindrical construction
- Bushing terminals designed for large cable connection and direct bus bar mounting for banking for rectangular construction
- Available in rectangular and cylindrical construction
- Optimized design to ensure low weight, compactness, and reliability
- Twin protection: Self-healing + Pressure Sensitive Disconnector (PSD)

General Technical Specifications SYSCAP

Rated capacitance	: 1μF TO 100μF
Tolerance on capacitance	: ±5%, ±10%, ±20% (Other values of capacitance tolerance can be provided on request)
Dissipation factor (Tan delta)	: </= 0.1% @100Hz
Rated Voltage (Un)	: 250 V; 300 V; 350 V; 370 V; 400 V; 420 V; 440 V; 450 V; 500 V
Rated Frequency	: 50 / 60 Hz.
Maximum operating temp.	: 85°C
Can material	: Aluminium;Nylon; PBT; Polypropylene
Dielectric	: Polypropylene (Self Healing –SH)
Termination	: Single fast-on;Double fast-on;Wire;Cable
Test voltage between terminals	: 1.75 x U_r (Rated) for 60 sec.
Test voltage between terminal and case	: 2 KV AC for 60 sec.
Ref. Standards	: IEC:EN 60252 (Motor Run Capacitor), UL 810 IEC:EN 1048 (Luminaire Capacitors) IS : 2993 IS : 1709 IS : 1569.

Fig 4.6.2 Technical specifications

CAPACITANCE (MFD)	250-300VAC		350-370VAC		400-440VAC		450-500VAC	
	D	H	D	H	D	H	D	H
1.0	25	52	25	52	25	52	25	52
2.0	25	52	25	52	25	52	25	52
3.0	25	52	25	52	27	52	27	52
4.0	25	52	25	52	30	52	30	52
5.0	25	52	27	52	35	55	35	55
6.0	27	52	27	52	35	55	35	73
7.5	27	52	30	55	35	73	35	73
10.0	30	55	35	55	35	73	40	73
11.5	35	55	35	73	40	73	45	73
12.0	35	55	35	73	40	73	45	73
12.5	35	55	35	73	40	73	45	73
15.0	35	73	40	73	40	73	45	73
18.0	35	73	40	73	45	73	40	94
20.0	40	73	45	73	45	73	45	94
25.0	40	73	45	73	40	94	45	94
30.0	40	94	40	94	45	94	45	120
35.0	45	73	45	94	45	120	50	120
36.0	45	73	45	94	45	120	50	120
40.0	45	94	45	94	45	120	50	120
45.0	45	94	45	120	50	120	54	120
50.0	45	94	45	120	50	120	54	120
55.0	45	94	45	120	50	120	57	120
60.0	45	94	50	120	54	120	57	120
70.0	50	94	50	120	54	120	57	120
80.0	50	94	50	120	54	120	57	120

THE SPECIFICATIONS CAN BE DIFFERENT BASED ON SPECIFIC CUSTOMER REQUIREMENTS.

ALL DIMENSIONS ARE IN MILLIMETERS.

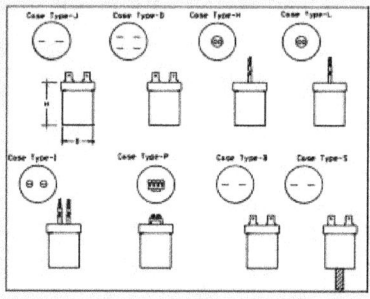

Fig 4.6.3 Specifications for P-100 series

4.6.1 SWOT ANALYSIS

While conducting strategic planning for any of the company it is useful to complete an analysis that takes into account not only your own business but also your competitors business and the current business well. The following description will highlight the strength, weakness, opportunity, and threats of the SSS Capacitors Pvt Ltd.

PORTERS 5 Forces Framework:

Since the company is competing internationally, it is necessary to consider the purchasing power of the rupee versus various international currencies, viz. Purchase Power Parity. According to Buffa (2), "to **compete effectively in a particular international market, we must be at least as productive in the field relative to our own economy as our international competitor is relative to its economy**". Hence productivity improvement takes on an even more important role in corporate strategy.

Further considerations pertain to the experience curve: the benefit obtained by getting on to a level experience curve is undermined by the rapidly changing technology in that product obsolescence would provide smaller returns in the maturity phase. This becomes more pronounced when large batch operations are introduced when a radical change in consumer tastes and obsolescence occur affecting the profitability.

STRENGTHS

Strengths: --- (what SSS capacitors Pvt. Ltd. does well), the following are some of the important strengths:

A leading capacitor manufacturing company in Karnataka

- Competitive price of products – the most powerful weapon of the company
- A Highly equipped and modern technological manufacturing plant
- Using good quality raw materials
- Sufficient human resource power
- Customer satisfaction through supplying products at in time
- Providing good services to regular customers for standard and non-standard products
- Skilled and highly experienced departmental heads

WEAKNESS

Areas where SSS capacitors has deficiency

- o The Capacity of the plant is not fully utilized
- o Due to fixed production lines, less scope exists for diversification of the products
- o Many Employees and workers are not satisfied with their work, salaries and temporary working nature
- o The company is not able to get enough grants from various financial institutions, depends on directors loans
- o A Lack of good relationship between the management and workers due to nonpermanent nature of work
- o There is no unity among the workers nor is there any organized worker union to deal with the management.

OPPORTUNITIES

- Growing power industry
- Availability of skilled workers and policy support
- Huge export opportunities and government support
- All types of industries try to minimum use energy, capacitors main function is to save the energy
- Having great opportunity to become a number one leading company in Asia
- Availability of well-connected road networks
- There is good scope for the company to grow in the present market because of the benefits given by the government to use capacitors.

THREATS

- These are factors that could damage the business
- Fluctuating policies of the government and ecological imbalance
- A radically innovative product design for standard and non-standard products
- Economic crisis and high cost for installation of plant

- Exchange rate threats and PPP effects
- Chinese and other SE Asian entries to the local market

MISSION

To be a leader in the field of development and manufacturing.
For this, the management is trying their level best to be consistent in quality, continual improvement and safety of company's operation and employees. The company works with a mission quality, efficiency and customer satisfaction, which is being met through teamwork and continual quality improvement.

VISION

Helps to India reduce consumption of power by providing better power factory correction deceives of production

To save the energy and increasing efficiency of working condition

Providing more number of employment opportunities

OBJECTIVES

Development of skilled personnel

Contribute towards HRD

Look after employees welfare

Reward for best performance

4.6.2 PESTLE ANALYSIS

The Pestle analysis is an extension of the SWOT analysis. PESTLE consists of

Tools used by marketing analysts to evaluate the changing environment in which the business operates. Hence it is a Tool of Strategic Management.

PESTLE stands for:

POLITICAL, ECONOMIC, SOCIAL, TECHNOLOGICAL LEGAL and ENVIRONMENTAL factors which could affect the business.

In more detail:

- **The political** situation of the country -- how it could affect the industry?
- Prevalent economic factors?
- Effect of culture in the market and its determinants? (**SOCIAL**)
- **Technological** innovations and effect on the market structure?
- **Legislations** and any change in the legislations?
- **Environmental** concerns for the industry? (Cost of Polluting, disposal of waste etc).

Michael Porter extended this to in more detail to evolve a **5 Force** structural matrix affecting the business:

1. Rivalry amongst firms

2. Threat of New Entrants

3. Threat of substitutes

4 Bargaining power of suppliers

5 Bargaining power of Buyers.

In relation to the capacitor industry particularly in the Southern Region, factor (1) is minimal since there are few competing firms here.

Factor (2) is possible but they would have to consider the dominant position enjoyed by SSS

3) Threat of substitutes—possible threat from radical new technology, but these would take a number of years to take effect

4) Bargaining power of suppliers – possible but SSS has undertaken in house manufacture of film, and aluminum cans to minimize this factor.

5) Bargaining power of Buyers—minimized by positioning SSS as one of the sole suppliers in the region.

4.7 CONCLUSION

The implementation of controls on quality appears to be dependent solely on machine automated checks. There is no scheme for manual and random checks. Control charts are not kept in the shop floor as in open view of machine operators.

Inventory control is also not done in real time, depending mainly on buffer stocks which lead to large wastage of floor area which could usefully be used for other activities and departments. The inventory buildup is also indicated in the parametric analysis of CCD.

Inventory is kept in storage and buffer stock held at various transfer and shipping locations, following a Push model, and not in conformance with JIT or Lean Manufacture.

Chapter V

Financial Analysis:

The health of the company may be ascertained by taking the financial "temperature" using certain parameters extracted from the Balance Sheet and other reports. What is given is as below:

IMPORTANT RATIOS

Gross Profit/Turnover= 24.38

Net Profit/Turnover=.75

Stock in trade to turnover= 1.94

Market consumed to finished goods= 82.15

From the Balance sheet the following ratios can be estimated:

Current Ratio= Current total ASSETS/Current total Liabilities= .812

Cash Ratio = Cash Balance/Current Liability = 2277024/155193840= 0.147

Quick Ratio = (Cash +Marketable securities+ Accounts receivable)/Current Liabilities =0.622

Dividend yield 4% (2015), 10% (2016)

The Ratios for a well-established firm in the same business (HAVELLS) are:

Current Ratio 1.89, Quick Ratio 1.58, dividend yield .68% (source moneycontrol.com, accessed Feb 2018)

For MURATA in Japan, the ratios are: Current Ratio = 2.79

Quick Ratio = 1.94

Dividend Yield 1.57% (source Investing.com accessed Feb 2018)

DUPONT IDENTITY

1) For 2016

ROE = (Net Profit/Net sales)* (Net Sales/ Avg Total Assets)* (Average T.A/Shareholder Equity)

= Net Profit/ SHE= 5626600/62363900=**.09**, (from P&L, Balance Sheet **2016**)

Whereas NP/NS=0.00151

NS/ATA= 1.2216

ATA/SHE= 56.171

By DUPONT = .1

2) From Balance Sheet 31 March 2015

Net Profit= 2014319

Net Sales = 330789887

Average Total Assets = 305362404

Share Holder Equity = 54363900

ROE= NP/SHE = 2014319/54363900= 0.037

Closing comments

Electric Power is the raw prime mover of Industry. Lack of Power causes a shortage of production, layoffs, and loss of revenue. Proper use of Capacitors reduces wastage of power and improves consumption efficiency. The Capacitor industry is closely connected with the electronic, electrical, IT and Mechanical Industries, including Military, communication and Aviation engineering sectors. Small and Medium Industries contribute to Self Reliance and add to the Nations GNP. Capacitors can be used in any sector where the power consumption is more, such as agriculture, cement, steel, tool making industries, Electricity distribution boards, big industrial areas, etc. These components also reduce accidents, short circuits, etc.

Competing in this field internationally requires that the producer be at least as productive in the field relative to his own economy as the international competitors are relative to their economies, Buffa and Sarin (2). The parity is further affected by the currency exchange ratio, and productivity.

ELECTRONIC INDUSTRY

Electronics is one of the fastest growing segments of the Indian industry. Today the electronics industry is completely delicensed, with the exception of aerospace.

The electronic industry in India constitutes less than 1% of the global market. The demand for these products, however, is growing rapidly and the investments are flowing in to augment the manufacturing capacity

Among manufacturing industries, the electronics industry occupies a key position in modern science and technology. It plays a vital role in the fields of atomic energy, communications, defense, education, entertainment and space technology. Until the 1970's the electronic industry was the most protected of all the Indian industries. The country's electronics policy strongly favored self-reliance and technology and capital imports were strongly discouraged. This resulted in the electronics industry being highly underdeveloped till the late 1980's. The industry was very inefficient, producing outdated and low quality models at a very high cost. For example, in the 1980's TV set manufacture was attempted by several private and state companies; however the cost and quality was far below that of imported sets, leading to a large black and grey market for these items. IC manufacture was also attempted, however till even recently major IC manufacturers have not invested in India, diverting instead to other regions in SE Asia.

The Electronic industry is a fast-growing sector in India, this sector starts from minute electronic items to large size transformers, capacitors etc, without the support of electronic instruments no industry can run. It also contributes to the improvement of the economic condition of the nation

India remains a major importer of electronic materials, components and finished equipment amounting to around $20 billion (Rs84000 crore now) in 2008. The country imports electronic goods mainly from China

In the last four years, production of computers has grown at a compounded annual growth rate (CAGR) of 31%, the highest among the various electronic products in India. This has been followed by communication and broadcast equipment (25%), strategic electronics (20%) and industrial electronics (17%).

India is the fifth largest economy in the world and has the second largest gross domestic product among the emerging economies. Owing to its large population, the potential consumer demand is ever increasing and consequently, under appropriate conditions, strong growth performance can be expected. The liberalization of the Indian economy that began in 1991 has started changing regulatory, financial, and monetary policies leading to a higher pace of growth. The electronics industry is already a world leader. Several new themed zones will make their debut in 2009, reflecting the latest technological developments in the fast-paced electronics industry, namely Computer & Peripherals, Digital Imaging, Electronic Gaming **and** Healthcare Electronics

During the course of study, it was found that,

- SSS is a growing company. It has good technical support from employees, who are all well qualified and also well-trained personnel
- A majority of the industry uses AC capacitors
- Majority of the capacitors are purchased by dedicated customers
- The company should give good training facilities to their employees
- The company has an automated modern manufacturing plant
- SSS capacitors strength is control of the regional market

SUGGESTIONS AND RECOMMENDATION

- The Company has to give preference to the six sigma concept
- Building the relationship between workers and management
- To Solve the employee's problems on a regular basis
- Human resource management should be properly organized
- Company should apply promotional activities in which advertising plays a crucial role, this could then boost the sales
- Providing recreational facility to the workers to reduce the boredom from long duration of work
- The company must substantiate the pricing of its product and use new technology
- The company uses only on-the-job training
- The company management personnel do not interact on the shop floor.
- Company must utilize the human resource and technological resource effectively

- SSS capacitors Pvt Ltd policy is to service continuously for improvement of their products, services and also to give quality products to their customer to increases their creditability in the field of capacitors
- Training is being conducted for the entire staff especially for the workers to train them in all the field for job rotation
- SSS capacitors has highly qualified and talented departmental heads that is specialized is advanced field of mechanical design, system engineering, and production technology
- SSS is having big market representation and a good customer relation with the help of the Public Sector industry in Bangalore
- SSS has established good network all over India and abroad
- To reach the global demand effectively, the company has to strengthen its functional areas
- Keeping in mind the increasing demand for quality products they have produced a wide range of capacitors

CHAPTER VI

Summary and Findings

IMPORTANT RATIOS AFFECTING PRODUCTION

Gross Profit/Turnover= 24.38

Net Profit/Turnover=.75

Stock in trade to turnover= 1.94

Market consumed to finished goods= 82.15

Supply Chain Metrics:

Material consumed to Finished Goods= Total Inventory/Annual sales =19/24*.365=.8215

TID = 300

DPO =Acounts payable/Value of Raw Materials consumed= 228

DSO= A/c receivables/annual sales = 83.5

CCD= TID+DS – DPO= 300+83.5-228=156

Approximately 2 turnovers per year.

The Return on Equity was about .04 (4 %) in 2015, whereas in 2016 it has increased to almost .1 or 10%.

Salary scales: The graphs of salaries vs level show an approximately exponential variation with level. The closest to a Pareto relationship is seen in the Production department salaries.

The regression gives for salary vs level x

Salary= 106989.97 exp(-.279 x), with a correlation coefficient of 96%

For the heads of all departments, excluding the CEO, one obtains:

Salary = 283767 exp (-.218 x) with a **correlation of 88%**

Without the CEO one gets

Salary= 148288 exp(-.157 x), **correlation 93.4%**

With a linear regression without CEO, one gets

Salary = 130382.9 -10900.8 x, correlation 92%

These regressions indicate that an equitable distribution of salary would have a top salary with approximately 148000 or 130000. The salary of the CEO is approximately **5 times** this from the regression in either case.

APPENDICES

SOLID STATE SYSTEMS PRIVATE LIMITED
HOSKOTE - 562114

Balance Sheet as at 31st March, 2015

Particulars	Note No	As at 31st March 2015	As at 31st March 2014
EQUITY AND LIABILITIES			
Shareholder's Funds			
Share Capital	1	543,63,900	495,13,900
Reserves and Surplus	2	170,34,857	153,37,611
Money received against share warrants			
Share application money pending allotment		20,00,000	-
Non-Current Liabilities			
Long term borrowings	3	70,47,118	182,96,299
Deferred tax liabilities (Net)	4	166,59,374	165,41,795
Other long term liabilities	5	37,67,496	-
Long term provisions	5A	9,89,328	4,82,362
Current Liabilities			
Short term borrowings	6	624,96,475	596,09,043
Trade payables	7	716,61,765	572,74,414
Other current liabilities	8	203,49,105	369,12,719
Short term provisions	9	6,86,493	12,90,970
TOTAL		**2570,55,911**	**2552,59,113**
ASSETS			
Non-current Assets			
Fixed assets	10		
Tangible assets		1216,33,320	1267,23,121
Intangible assets		6,28,276	8,79,659
Capital work-in-progress		21,529	21,529
Intangible assets under development		9,55,000	9,55,000
Non-current investments	11	500	-
Deferred tax assets (net)		-	-
Long term loans and advances	12	77,62,689	73,02,204
Other non-current assets	13	-	73,305
Current Assets			
Current investments		-	-
Inventories	14	351,20,821	351,69,596
Trade receivables	15	745,96,523	657,62,838
Cash and Bank balances	16	22,77,024	63,34,598
Short-term loans and advances	17	119,91,027	75,99,269
Other current assets	18	20,69,202	44,37,994
TOTAL		**2570,55,911**	**2552,59,113**

Significant Accounting Policies and Notes on accounts   27

See accompanying notes to the Financial Statements

For Dagliya & Co.
Chartered Accountants
FRN: 0671S

P.MANOHARA GUPTA
Partner   M.No. 16444
PLACE : BANGALORE
DATE : 4.9.2015

FOR SOLID STATE SYSTEMS PVT. LTD

(JAWAD BASITH)   (OMER BASITH)
DIRECTOR   DIRECTOR

BALANCE SHEET 2015

40: Accounting Ratios

		Current year amount	Ratio to turnover(%)	Last year amount	Last year %
1	Total turnover of the assessee	33,07,89,887		30,32,39,608	
2	Gross profit/turnover	8,06,32,096	24.38	7,57,14,873	24.97
3	Net profit/turnover	24,67,605	0.75	83,19,690	2.74
4	Stock-in-trade/turnover	64,16,392	1.94	81,89,334	2.7
5	Material consumed to Finished goods		82.15		78.28
	Material consumed	19,93,47,458		17,29,40,888	
	Finished goods	24,26,73,272		22,09,27,106	

41: Indirect tax Demands / refunds

Financial Year	Relevant Tax law	Type	Demand / Refund Date	Amount	Remarks
2014-15	Central Excise Act	Refund	31-Dec-2014	3,32,171	
2014-15	Central Excise Act	Refund	23-Jan-2015	4,47,689	
2014-15	Central Excise Act	Refund	23-Jan-2015	15,06,209	
2012-13	VAT Act- Karnataka	Refund	26-Aug-2014	14,25,119	
2013-14	VAT Act- Karnataka	Refund	28-Feb-2015	19,84,680	
2012-13	Other: CST	Demand	30-Jul-2014	42,222	

For Dagliya & Co. Chartered Accountants

P M GUPTA
Partner, M. No. 016444
Firm reg. No. 000671S

Place: BANGALORE
Date: **29-09-2015**

Balance Sheet as at 31st March., 2016

Particulars	Note No.	As at 31st March 2016	As at 31st March 2015
EQUITY AND LIABILITIES			
Shareholder's Funds			
Share Capital	1	52,363,900	54,363,900
Reserves and Surplus	2	2,661,457	17,034,857
Money received against share warrants			
Share application money pending allotment			2,000,000
Non-Current Liabilities			
Long term borrowings	3	10,890,947	7,047,118
Deferred tax liabilities (Net)	4	17,232,375	16,659,374
Other long term liabilities			
Long term provisions	5	5,342,940	4,758,924
Current Liabilities			
Short term borrowings	6	53,952,647	62,496,475
Trade payables	7		
(i)Total outstanding dues of micro enterprises and small enterprises		30,062,933	9,566,480
(ii)Total outstanding dues of creditors other than micro enterprises and small		54,069,406	62,095,285
Other current liabilities	8	17,669,102	19,504,162
Short term provisions	9	3,207,077	1,541,436
TOTAL		**305,362,404**	**257,059,911**
ASSETS			
Non-current Assets			
Fixed assets	10		
Tangible assets		116,749,525	121,633,320
Intangible assets		376,853	628,276
Capital work-in-progress		21,529	21,529
Intangible assets under development		4,115,715	956,000
Non-current investments	11	500	500
Deferred tax assets (net)			
Long term loans and advances	12	9,536,313	7,762,689
Other non-current assets	13		
Current Assets			
Current investments			
Inventories	14	45,738,405	55,116,231
Trade receivables	15	112,427,974	74,596,523
Cash and bank balances	16	3,740,531	2,277,004
Short term loans and advances	17	9,194,473	11,951,023
Other current assets	18	3,462,687	2,069,202
TOTAL		**305,362,404**	**257,085,911**

Significant Accounting Policies and Notes on accounts

See accompanying notes to the Financial Statements

For Dagliya & Co.
Chartered Accountants
FRN. 06710

P.MANOHARA GUPTA
Partner   M.No. 16444

TOP SOLID STATE SYSTEMS PVT. LTD.

DIRECTOR   DIRECTOR

Place : Bangalore
Date

Balance sheet 2016

SALARY SCALE

DESIGNATION	GROSS
CEO	574250
EXECUTIVE ASST TO CEO	48210.00

<table>
<tr><td rowspan="20" style="writing-mode: vertical">MARKETING</td><td colspan="2">MARKETING DEPARTMENT</td></tr>
<tr><td>DESIGNATION</td><td>GROSS</td></tr>
<tr><td>MARKETING HEAD</td><td>109900.00</td></tr>
<tr><td>MANAGER-EXPORTS</td><td>39735.00</td></tr>
<tr><td>MARKETING EXECUTIVE</td><td>25963.00</td></tr>
<tr><td>ENGINEER SALES & MKTG</td><td>30380.00</td></tr>
<tr><td>MKTG SALES COORDINATOR</td><td>12500.00</td></tr>
<tr><td colspan="2">COIMBATORE BRANCH MARKETING</td></tr>
<tr><td>DESIGNATION</td><td>GROSS</td></tr>
<tr><td>BRANCH MANAGER (COIMBATORE)</td><td>24228.00</td></tr>
<tr><td>MARKETING EXECUTIVE</td><td>21148.00</td></tr>
<tr><td colspan="2">MUMBAI BRANCH MARKETING</td></tr>
<tr><td>DESIGNATION</td><td>GROSS</td></tr>
<tr><td>BUSINESS MANAGER (MUMBAI)</td><td>42512.00</td></tr>
<tr><td colspan="2">FARIDABAD BRANCH MARKETING</td></tr>
<tr><td>DESIGNATION</td><td>GROSS</td></tr>
<tr><td>BUSINESS MANAGER (FARIDABAD)/ COMMISSION AGENT</td><td>0.00</td></tr>
<tr><td>MARKETING EXECUTIVE (FARIDABAD)</td><td>18380.00</td></tr>
</table>

ACCOUNTS & FINANCE DEPARTMENT	
DESIGNATION	**GROSS**
GM COMMERCIAL	113720.00
ACCOUNTS SENIOR ASST	26419.00
EXECUTIVE-FINANCE	29680.00
ACCOUNTS ASST	13403.00

PURCHASE DEPARTMENT	
DESIGNATION	**GROSS**
MANAGER-PURCHASE	44752.00
ASST MANAGER PURCHASE	27037.00
PURCHASE ASST	10000.00

STORES DEPARTMENT	
DESIGNATION	GROSS
MANAGER STORES	46395.00
STORES ASST	9000.00

PRODUCTION & PLANNING DEPARTMENT	
DESIGNATION	GROSS
PPC MANAGER	48210.00
PPC EXECUTIVE	15000.00
PPC ASST	10000.00

PRODUCTION DEPARTMENT	
DESIGNATION	GROSS
GM-PRODUCTION	99405.00
MANAGER PRODUCTION	62388.00
PRODUCTION ENGINEER	24269.00
PRODUCTION SUPERVISOR	18500.00
MANAGER ALUMINUM DEPT	27125.00
SUPERVISOR RESIN DEPT	22934.00
METALISATION MAINTENANCE INCHARGE	42616.00
SUPERVISOR WINDING	21267.00

QUALITY DEPARTMENT	
DESIGNATION	GROSS
DGM QC	122140.00
ENGINEER-Q/C	22426.00
R & D ASST QC	15000.00
ENGINEERING ASST	10000.00
R & D ASST QC	10000.00

MAINTENANCE DEPARTMENT	
DESIGNATION	GROSS
MANAGER MAINTENANCE	44624.00
MAINTENANCE ASST	16400.00
MAINTENANCE ELECTRICIAN	9500.00

ADMIN DEPARTMENT	
DESIGNATION	GROSS
MANAGER ADMIN	43711.00

EXECUTIVE-EXIM	31427.00

HR DEPARTMENT	
DESIGNATION	**GROSS**
HR MANAGER	20488.00

COMPANY INCENTIVE AND BONUS

L O	DESIGNATION	GROSS	ANNUAL GROSS	PERFOR MANCE BONUS %	PERFORMANCE BONUS %
1	BRANCH MANAGER (COIMBATORE)	24228	290736	8.5	24713
2	MARKETING EXECUTIVE	21148	253776	8.5	21571
3	GM COMMERCIAL	113720	1364640	16.5	225166
4	ASST MANAGER PURCHASE	27037	324444	8.5	27578
5	MANAGER STORES	46395	556740	8.5	47323
6	PPC MANAGER	48210	578520	16.5	95456
7	MANAGER PRODUCTION	62388	748656	16.5	123528
8	PRODUCTION ENGINEER	24269	291228	16.5	48053
9	PRODUCTION SUPERVISOR	18500	222000	8.5	18870
10	METALISATION MAINTENANCE INCHARGE	42616	511392	8.5	43468
11	ENGINEER-Q/C	22426	269112	8.5	22875
12	HR MANAGER	20488	245856	8.5	20898
			TOTAL		719497

Charge ID	Creation Date	Modification Date	Closure Date	Assets Under Charge	Amount		Charge Holder
1023415 3	2010-07-21	-	2013-11-18	Immovable property or any interest therein; Movable property (not being pledge)	10,000,000		KARNATAKA STATE FINANCIAL CORPORATION
1039578 4	2012-12-24	2013-07-29	-		7,500,000		KARNATAKA STATE FINANCIAL CORPORATION
1044909 7	2013-07-29	-	2015-11-05	Book debts; Movable property (not being pledge)	10,000,000		KARNATAKA STATE FINANCIAL CORPORATION
8006223 1	1994-02-01	-	2011-02-25	Movable property (not being pledge)	2,000,000		INDUSTRIAL CREDIT AND DEVELOPMENT SYNDICATE LTD
8006223 2	1994-02-07	-	2011-03-25	Movable property (not being pledge)	146,000		CITI BANK
90193053	1973-02-26	-	2013-10-21			70,000	STATE BANK OF INDIA
90193146	1983-09-07	-	2013-10-21	Book debts	1,780,000		STATE BANK OF INDIA
90193301	1987-06-06	2016-06-18	-	Immovable property or any interest therein; Book debts; Floating charge; Movable property (not being pledge)	114,600,000		State Bank of India
90193932	1995-08-	-	2011-01-			66,000	ANZ

Charge ID	Creation Date	Modification Date	Closure Date	Assets Under Charge	Amount	Charge Holder
	30			17		GRINDALYAS BANK
90194071	1997-01-29	1997-01-29	2013-11-06		8,000,000	KARNATAKA STATE FINANCIAL CORPORATION
90194396	2002-06-29	-	2010-08-09		491,040	SUNDARAM AUTO FINANCE
100059656	2016-10-07	-	-	Book debts; Movable property (not being pledge)	5,000,000	KARNATAKA STATE FINANCIAL CORPORATION

Establishments Details

Establishment Name	City	Pincode	Address
SOLID STATE SYSTEMS PVT.LTD.,	KRPURAMWHITE FIELD	562114	RAHATH BAGH, 8A-1,KIADB INDL.AREA OLD MADRAS ROAD,HOSKOTE657KN

SOLID STATE SYSTEMS PRIVATE LIMITED
HOSAKOTE - 562114
Statement of Profit and Loss for the year ended 31st March, 2015

Particulars	Note No	Figures for the current reporting period	Figures for the previous reporting period
I. Revenue from operations (Gross)	19	3538,03,663	3243,06,619
Less: Excise Duty		230,13,776	210,67,011
Revenue from operations (Net)		3307,89,887	3032,39,608
II. Other Income	20	14,52,077	20,86,689
III. Total Revenue (I +II)		3322,41,964	3053,26,297
IV. Expenses:			
Cost of materials consumed	21	1865,66,759	1673,87,692
Purchase of Stock-in-Trade - Capacitors		6,55,855	5,60,760
Changes in inventories of finished goods, work-in-progress and Stock-in-Trade	22	(12,30,985)	92,88,829
Employee benefit expense	23	525,43,255	434,05,147
Financial costs	24	167,34,739	184,18,296
Depreciation and amortization expense	25	99,60,403	89,90,978
Other expenses	26	644,47,890	489,49,599
Total Expenses		3296,77,916	2970,01,301
V. Profit before exceptional and extraordinary items and tax	(III - IV)	25,64,048	83,24,996
VI. Exceptional items			
Prior Period (Expense) / Income		(96,443)	(5,306)
VII. Profit before extraordinary items and tax (V + VI)		24,67,605	83,19,690
VIII. Extraordinary Items			
IX. Profit before tax (VII - VIII)		24,67,605	83,19,690
X. Tax expense:			
(1) Current tax		5,00,000	15,85,320
(2) Deferred tax		2,59,367	4,26,807
(3) MAT Credit Entitlement		(4,77,879)	(15,39,140)
(4) Tax Adjustment for earlier years		1,71,797	9,05,861
XI. Profit(Loss) from the perid from continuing operations	(IX-X)	20,14,319	69,40,842
XII. Profit/(Loss) from discontinuing operations			
XIII. Tax expense of discounting operations			
XIV. Profit/(Loss) from Discontinuing operations (XII - XIII)			
XV. Profit/(Loss) for the period (XI + XIV)		20,14,319	69,40,842
XVI. Earning per equity share:			
(1) Basic		4.04	15.84
(2) Diluted		4.04	15.84

Significant Accounting Policies and Notes on accounts   27
See accompanying notes to the Financial Statements

For Dagliya & Co.
Chartered Accountants
FRN: 0671S

P. MANOHARA GUPTA
Partner   M.No. 16444
PLACE : BANGALORE
DATE : 4.9.2015

FOR SOLID STATE SYSTEMS PVT. LTD

(JAWAD BASITH)   (OMER BASITH)
DIRECTOR   DIRECTOR

Profit Loss 2016

Statement of Profit and Loss for the year ended 31st March, 2016

Particulars	Note No	Figures for the current reporting period	Figures for the previous reporting period
I. Revenue from operations (Gross)	15	409,443,008	353,803,663
Less: Excise Duty		32,569,403	23,013,776
Revenue from operations (Net)		376,873,605	330,789,887
II. Other Income	20	935,000	1,452,077
III. Total Revenue (I +II)		377,808,605	332,241,964
IV. EXPENSES			
Cost of materials consumed	21	209,623,561	186,566,769
Purchase of Semi Finished - Capacitors		2,867,193	
Purchase of Stock-in-Trade - Capacitors		1,431,183	655,855
Changes in inventories of finished goods, work-in-progress and Stock-in-Trade	22	(1,366,741)	(1,230,985)
Employee benefit expense	23	57,323,279	52,543,255
Financial costs	24	13,968,953	18,734,739
Depreciation and amortization expense	25	9,944,131	9,960,403
Other expenses	26	77,375,703	64,447,890
Total Expenses		371,142,365	329,677,915
V. Profit before exceptional and extraordinary items and tax (III - IV)		6,666,240	2,564,048
VI. Exceptional items			
Prior Period (Expenses) / Income			(96,443)
Profit/(Loss) on sale of fixed assets		(333,901)	
VII. Profit before extraordinary items and tax (V + VI)		6,332,339	2,467,605
VIII. Extraordinary items			
IX. Profit before tax (VII - VIII)		6,332,339	2,467,605
X. Tax expense:			
(1) Current tax		1,300,000	500,000
(2) Deferred tax		593,001	259,367
(3) MAT Credit Entitlement		(1,216,500)	(477,879)
(4) Tax adjustment for earlier years		29,438	171,797
XI. Profit/(Loss) from the period from continuing operations (IX-X)		5,626,600	7,014,319
XII. Profit/(Loss) from discontinuing operations			
XIII. Tax expense of discontinuing operations			
XIV. Profit/(Loss) from Discontinuing operations (XII - XIII)			
XV. Profit/(Loss) for the period (XI + XIV)		5,626,600	7,014,319
XVI. Earning per equity share of Rs. 100 Each			
(1) Basic		9.99	4.04
(2) Diluted		9.99	4.04

Significant Accounting Policies and Notes on accounts — 27
See accompanying notes to the Financial Statements

For Daglity & Co
Chartered Accountants
FRN 0671S

P.MANOHARA GUPTA
Partner   M.No. 16444

Place : Bangalore
Date :

FOR SOLID STATE SYSTEMS PVT. LTD

(IQBAL BASITH)   (OMER BASITH)
DIRECTOR   DIRECTOR

BIBLIOGRAPHY

1. F.W. Taylor, **Scientific Management**, comprising *Shop Management*, *The Principles of Scientific Management* and Testimony Before the Special House Committee, Harper & Row, 1911

2. E.S. Buffa and R.K.Sarin "Modern Production/Operations Management", 8th Edn, John Wiley 1987

3. Gilbreth, Frank Bunker. *Primer of scientific management.* D. Van Nostrand Company, 1912.

4. P.J. Kolesar, "Juran's Lectures to Japanese Executives in 1954: A Perspective and Some Contemporary Lessons", Quality Management Journal Vol. 15, Iss. 3, 2008

5 B. Mahadevan "Operations Management", Pearson 2015

6. S Eilon "Elements of Production Planning and Control", 1989, Universal Bombay

7. D. Hoffman," The hierarchy of Supply Chain Metrics: Diagnosing your supply chain Health", AMR Research Report, Feb 18, 2004

8. M R A Anvari, MD Nazari, S M Razavi,"How to Measure Supply Chain Performance", Intl Review of Business Res. Papers.V 712, March 2011,p230-244

9. B.M.Beamon, " Measuring Supply Chain Performance", Intl Jnl of Operations and Production Management, v19,3,1999,p 275-292

10. A Gunasekharan, C Patel, E Tirtoglu ," Performance Measures and metrics in a Supply Chan Environment", Intl Jnl of Operations and Prodn Management, 21, no ½, 2001

11. A Gunasekharan, C Patel, R E McGaughey, " A Framework for Supply Chain Management", Intl Jnl. of Production Economics", 8,7, 2004,p 333-347

12. N Gamme and M Johanssen, "Measuring Supply Chain Performance through KPI identification and evaluation", Report e 2015:109, Chalmers Univ.

13. J R P Hammesfahn, J A Pope, A Ardalan," Strategic Planning fr Production Capacity", Intl Jnl of Operations and Prodn.Mgmt, 13(5), 1993,pp41-53

14. L Abuhilal, G R Rabadi, A Souza- Poza, "Supply Chain Inventory control: A Comparison Among JIT, MRP and MRP with Information Sharing using Simulation", Engg Mgmt Jnl, V18,2, July 2006, p51-57

15. F Dooley "Logistics, Inventory Control and SCM", Choices, 20(4),2005

\16. F. Constantino, G DiGrazio, A Sharban, M Trovier, "Inventory Control system based on control charts to improve supply chain performances", Int Jnl of Simul Model, 13,3, 2014,263-275

17. Dar El Mansoor (1973) " MALB – a heuristic technique for balancing large scale single model Assembly Lines" AIIE Transactions, 5,(4).p 343-356

18 Gunther R E, Johnson G D, and Peterson R S, (1983) "Currently practiced formulations of the assembly line balancing Problem", J. Op Mgmt., 3 (4), 209-221

19 D Sharma, D Sharma, JP Sharma, "Production Planning and Control", IJSRET 3,3, 2014

20 T T Paterson "Job evaluation", Business Books, 1972

21 Graicunas, V.A., "Relationship in Organization (pp. 183-187) in *Papers on the Science of Administration*, edited by Luther Gulick and Lyndal F. Urwick, published by Columbia University's Institute of Public Administration in 1937.

22 Urwick, L.E. (1956) "The Manager's span of control", *Harvard Business Review*, May/June 1956.

23 Joan Woodward, Industrial Organization: Theory and Practice, OUP, 1965

24 D Babcock and L C Morse "Managing Engineering and Technology", PHI, 2006

25 Ouchi, W. and Dowling, J. (1974) "Defining Span of Control", *Administrative Sciences Quarterly*, Vol 19, 1974.

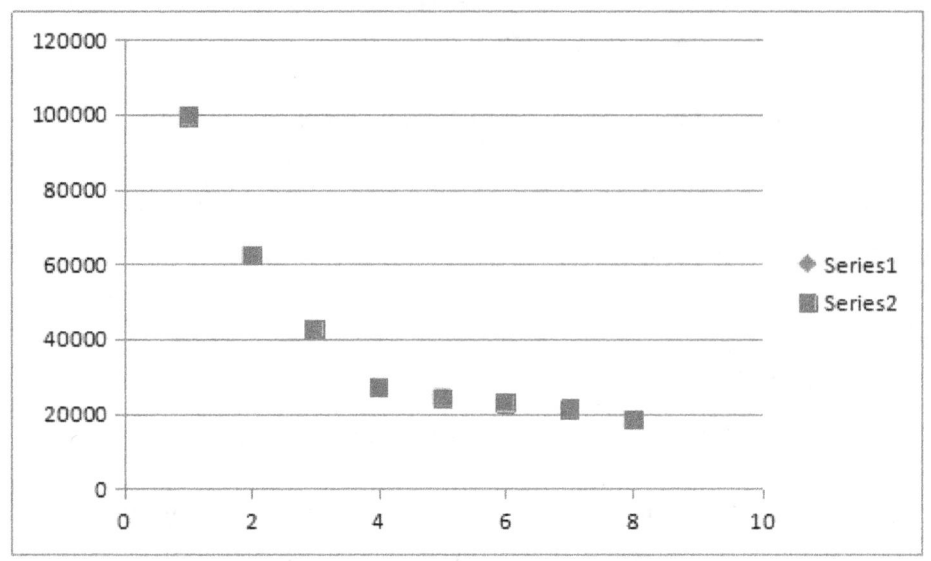

5.1. PRODUCTION DEPARTMENT SALARIES vs LEVEL

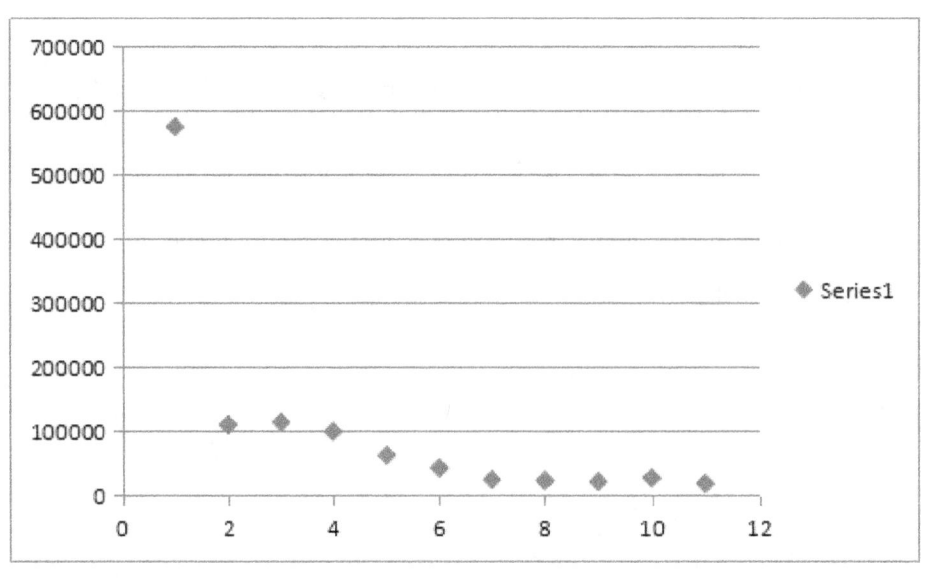

5.2. SALARIES FOR HEADS OF VARIOUS DEPARTMENTS vs LEVEL

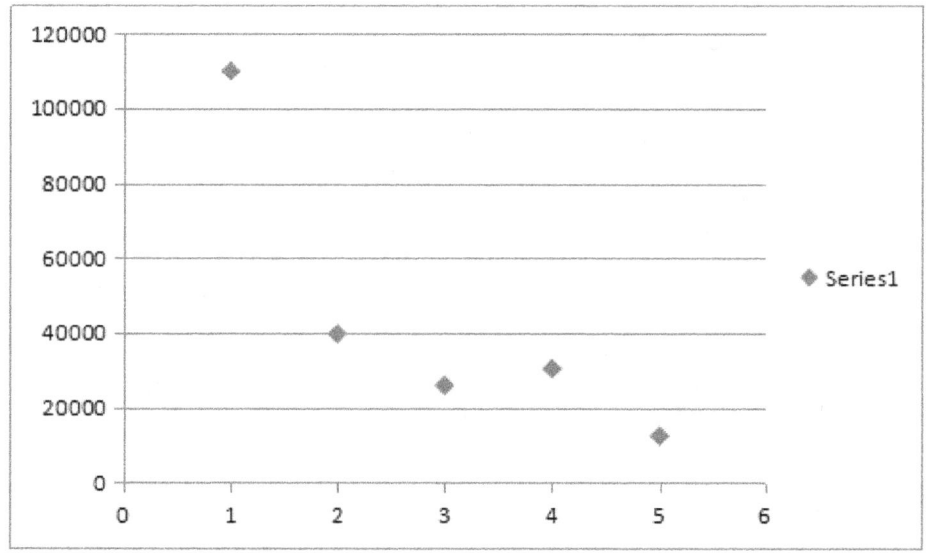

5.3 Marketing department salaries versus level

www.ingramcontent.com/pod-product-compliance
Lightning Source LLC
Chambersburg PA
CBHW082147230526
45467CB00043B/2403